Multiple Use
Job Descriptions

Recent Titles from Quorum Books

Exceptional Entrepreneurial Women: Strategies for Success
Russel R. Taylor

Collective Bargaining and Impasse Resolution in the Public Sector
David A. Dilts and William J. Walsh

New Directions in MIS Management: A Guide for the 1990s
Robert J. Thierauf

The Labor Lawyer's Guide to the Rights and Responsibilities
of Employee Whistleblowers
Stephen M. Kohn and Michael D. Kohn

Strategic Organization Planning: Downsizing for Survival
David C. Dougherty

Joint Venture Partner Selection: Strategies for Developed Countries
J. Michael Geringer

Sustainable Corporate Growth: A Model and Management Planning Tool
John J. Clark, Thomas C. Chiang, and Gerard T. Olson

Competitive Freedom Versus National Security Regulation
Manley Rutherford Irwin

Labor Law and Business Change: Theoretical and Transactional Perspectives
Samuel Estreicher and Daniel G. Collins, eds.

The Constitutional Right to a Speedy and Fair Criminal Trial
Warren Freedman

Entrepreneurial Systems for the 1990s: Their Creation, Structure, and Management
John E. Tropman and Gersh Morningstar

From Organizational Decline to Organizational Renewal:
The Phoenix Syndrome
Mary E. Guy

Modern Analytical Auditing: Practical Guidance for Auditors and Accountants
Thomas E. McKee

Multiple Use Job Descriptions

A GUIDE TO ANALYSIS, PREPARATION, AND APPLICATIONS FOR HUMAN RESOURCES MANAGERS

Philip C. Grant

QUORUM BOOKS
New York • Westport, Connecticut • London

Library of Congress Cataloging-in-Publication Data

Grant, Philip C.
    Multiple use job descriptions : a guide to analysis, preparation,
and applications for human resources managers / Philip C. Grant.
        p.   cm.
    Bibliography: p.
    Includes index.
    ISBN 0-89930-416-8 (lib. bdg. : alk. paper)
    1. Job descriptions. I. Title.
HF5549.5.J613G73   1989
658.3′06—dc19   88-23664

British Library Cataloguing in Publication Data is available.

Library of Congress Catalog Card Number: 88-23664

ISBN: 0-89930-416-8

First published in 1989 by Quorum Books

Greenwood Press, Inc.
88 Post Road West, Westport, Connecticut 06881

Printed in the United States of America

∞™

The paper used in this book complies with the
Permanent Paper Standard issued by the National
Information Standards Organization (Z39.48-1984).

10 9 8 7 6 5 4 3 2 1

Contents

Preface

This book was designed as a specialized reference on job descriptions—how to prepare them and how to use them. Managers in any type of organization, personnel administrators and specialists in human resource management, and students in the field of human resource administration should find the book of real practical value.

The volume breaks new ground on a number of fronts. First, it identifies a far more extensive array of uses for job descriptions than any other book—132 major management uses are discussed. Second, it develops important points on how to gather data for job descriptions, heretofore neglected by the literature. Third, it emphasizes the importance of developing task/responsibility categories as an aid to understanding the design of work. Fourth, the book shows that the design of jobs can be accurately depicted by job descriptions only if attention is given to key unconventional types of job description information such as task times and priorities, non-work and semi-work activity, and unplanned work. And fifth, the book provides a comprehensive compilation of the most common problems associated with the preparation and use of job descriptions.

Acknowledgments

The author wishes to thank the following organizations and individuals for their considerable and much appreciated help in providing data for the book and in preparing the manuscript. The Jasper Wyman and Son Company helped by providing an opportunity for the author to test, firsthand, some of the job analysis techniques discussed in the book. The Greater Bangor Personnel Association helped by participating in an extensive research project that provided data on job description uses. Students in the author's spring 1987 Personnel Administration course contributed by gathering data about job description preparation practices and job description usage in various companies, both public and private. The author's wife, Kathy Grant, provided much help in proofreading the manuscript. Suzanne Bruce typed numerous drafts of various parts of the book. Sue McLaughlin did a super job typing and proofreading the final manuscript. All these people put considerable efforts into making this book a reality.

Multiple Use
Job Descriptions

CHAPTER 1

Job Descriptions: Their Nature and Importance

Job descriptions have enjoyed varying degrees of popularity over the years, with perhaps the height of their popularity coming during and shortly after World War I, as organizations grew rapidly in size and sought means for making large aggregations of resources manageable and efficient. In the mid-1960s and early 1970s job descriptions were shunned somewhat as people began to see them as primarily a symbol of bureaucracy and essentially a constraint on normal employee growth and development, as well as a factor limiting what management could do in the organization in response to demands for rapid change.

No one format and style for job descriptions have ever been widely accepted. They still come in all colors, shapes, and sizes in the practicing world. Sometimes they are highly elaborate documents. At other times they paint a portrait of the job in very few simple sentences. Often different types of formats and styles are found for job descriptions within a given organization. Most organizations do not do a very good job of preparing job descriptions.

Job descriptions are used by all types of organizations in various ways and to different degrees. Some organizations do not use them at all. Large organizations tend to use them more than do small organizations. Many organizations get excited about them at one point in time and then forget about them for extended periods until they come on hard times, for example, and experience a critical need for control. Most organizations do not understand the potential value of job descriptions and consequently highly underutilize them. The real tragedy comes in the many organizations that misunderstand what job descriptions are and consequently misuse them. The thrust of this chapter will be to identify clearly what job descriptions are and to emphasize, in general, why they are valuable.

WHAT JOB DESCRIPTIONS ARE

To understand and appreciate the job description (JD) it is useful to describe it in different ways from different angles:

A written display. A job description is a written display (paper document, computer screen image, blackboard presentation, etc.) explicitly describing what an employee does in the organization. It communicates to the reader what the job is like. It includes information about the employee's job but its focus is on depicting the duties and responsibilities the employee is expected to execute for the organization. A sample job description is presented in Appendix A. When such a written display is prepared for each position in the organization instead of for each class of similar positions (a job) it is often, and probably more appropriately, called a position description. In this book it will not be necessary to make this distinction. The term *job* will be used throughout all ensuing discussions.

A model of work design. A JD is a model of the design of the work performed by the employee. When properly developed it profiles the major components of a job's structure. It will generally not attempt to cover *all* facets of a job's design. To describe everything about a job is not necessary and indeed is impossible since jobs contain unplanned components—necessary but unforeseeable engagements. Also, trying to describe a job in great detail may require too costly an effort.

Key elements of the intrinsic (task) makeup of the job and of the physical and social environments in which the tasks are performed are generally included in the JD model. How the job relates, administratively and operationally, to other jobs in the organizational system is an element of structure usually identified in the model. Also, certain kinds of relationships among different tasks are often implied if not displayed explicitly in the JD.

A work plan. A job description is a work plan—a "map" that shows direction. As a plan it shows that the work the employee engages in has been thought through in a rational, conscious fashion—anticipated in advance of execution. As a plan it shows that work is not left to chance. It shows work is not something that is largely spontaneous. As a plan it shows that somebody has engaged in the considered evaluation of alternatives—that deliberate choices about what the employee does in the organization have been made. Moreover, as a plan the JD serves to bound, or constrain, employee activity in the organization. One is expected to conform to the plan, not to vault into any duty domain that might suit the fancy.

A role prescription. The job description is (or should be) a role prescription. It should not describe what the worker does if this is not what the organization wishes the worker to do. JDs must prescribe—spell out those duties (tasks) and responsibilities in which the organization thinks the employee should engage. JDs must never become simple written reflections of whatever employees actually do. The JD is the standard. It defines a pattern of behavior expectations. Actual behavior must be compared with this prescription for control purposes.

The term *role* is significant here too, and it has a broader connotation than the term *job*. The word *job* usually connotes simply a set of tasks operative and/or managerial—but, nonetheless, tasks. The concept of role incorporates such notions as work relations with others, justification for existence of the position, the impact of one's behavior in the position on the other workers, as well as when, where, and with what resources tasks should be performed. It implies that a number of features of one's work world need to be identified and understood if JDs are to serve as a useful management tool.

An "attachment" to the position. The JD attaches to the position not the person. An employee may perform the tasks incorporated in a number of different positions. This can happen when staffing for certain positions cannot be found, or when workers are out sick or on vacation. One employee may have to cover other positions while performing his or her own regular job; but the employee's job does not change during this effort. The job stays the same. It is just that now the employee has other jobs to fill in addition to the regular. Separate JDs should exist for each different position (job) the employee covers. The organization should not rely on just one document to cover the spectrum of this employee's activities.

Just as one person usually plays one role but on occasion may play multiple roles, a given role is usually played by one person but on occasion, such as with shift work, multiple individuals may take turns playing a role. There need be only one JD for the *role*, not multiple JDs for the multiple persons.

A picture of human resource investment. The job description shows what the organization's investment in the human resource is for. It is an expression of organizational need. It shows how the human resource should be utilized. It shows how that resource is to contribute to the organization's output. It shows any interested reader what the organization should be getting for what it gives out in paychecks. It is, in a broad sense, something like a contract with the employee, spelling out what demands the organization makes on the employee in exchange for giving the employee rewards such as pay, benefits, and such.

WHAT JOB DESCRIPTIONS ARE NOT

To fully understand and appreciate the JD it helps to look at what the JD is not:

Not a person specification. A job description is not a person specification or, more commonly called, a job specification. A person spec details the kinds and levels of skills, abilities, knowledge, and so on one must possess in order to do the job well or up to standard. Usually qualifications—experience and educational requirements—are specified in person specs. These requirements spell out the kinds and amounts of experience and training needed by employees if they are to acquire the skills, knowledge, and abilities necessary to perform at standard.

A person specification describes the kind of person needed to do the job. A JD, on the other hand, describes the nature of the work to be done. In practice, person specifications are often included in the same document with the description of the work. But the reader should recognize the distinction here and at least conceptually separate the two. See Appendix B for a sample person specification.

Not a description of how. A JD is not a procedure or methods description. Written procedures and methods present the steps to follow in accomplishing something. Procedures and methods show *how* to execute duties and responsibilities. The JD shows *what* to do but not how. See Appendix C for a sample procedure and a sample method.

Not a performance evaluation instrument. The JD is not a performance level assessment device. It does not specify performance criteria (ways to measure performance) nor does it specify performance standards (desired levels of performance). The JD shows *what* the worker is supposed to do. *How well* it is done is determined with a performance evaluation instrument that is best distinguished from, and kept separate from, the JD. Such instruments are used to measure the quantity, quality, timeliness, and cost of one's performance.

Sometimes JDs do identify key outcomes—results expected—or accountabilities; but specification of such is not a substitute for a fully developed performance assessment instrument. Doing this does aid in developing a performance assessment instrument, however. See Appendix D for a sample performance evaluation instrument.

Not a set of rules, regulations, policies, or proper practices. The JD is not a set of rules, regulations, policies, or proper practices. These specify acceptable and unacceptable behavior, or provide guidelines for doing the work and making decisions relative to the work. For example, good health and safety practices, or management policies on striving for a quality product, should not show up in the JD. The JD identifies what the work is. Rules, regulations, policies, and desired practices should be in separate documents. See Appendix E for sample rules, regulations, and policies.

Not an employment contract. A JD is not an employment contract, though as mentioned earlier it has similarities. Employment contracts may incorporate JDs, or refer to JDs, but JDs alone are not contracts, and must not be treated as contracts, with all those inherent rigidities. No JD can ever cover *all* demands that the organization may have to place on the worker. Things change. Organizations need flexibility in their usage of the human resource. Outside forces may influence an organization to completely change an employee's job overnight. Treating the JD as a work contract covering a required duration of time is dangerous. It excessively limits the capacity of the organization to adapt.

Not a set of objectives or goals. A JD is not a set of job objectives or goals. Job objectives and goals are formulated *from* the JD to assure their relevance and validity. But objectives are targets with measurable levels of accomplishments and time frames for accomplishment. Objectives are specific *results* to be achieved at some point in time. See Appendix F for a set of sample objectives.

Not a work schedule. A JD is not a work schedule. A well-written JD indicates how much time one should spend on different tasks but it does not tell precisely when specific tasks are to be done. The JD may, however, make general implications of when tasks are to be done or give broad time frames for accomplishment. For example, it may point out certain tasks be done during certain seasons or during a particular part of the year, but it is inappropriate to build into the JD weekly and daily task scheduling. Other documents should be used for this.

Not a description of informal organization and behavior. The JD does not focus on describing informal work, social, political, and other relations and behaviors with which workers typically are involved. The JD's emphasis is on planned, formalized, anticipated work roles and behaviors. The informal structures and processes that emerge spontaneously in any organizational setting may be elaborately described with appropriate sociometric techniques, but the JD is not the place for this material. As discussed later in Chapter 3, some reference to the informal system is often appropriate in a JD in the non-work/semi-work activity category.

Not a picture of rewards. JDs do not describe reward structures and privileges that employees experience. Salary levels and grades, benefits, time off for good attendance, and so on, should be highlighted in separate documents designed to disclose what the organization gives employees in exchange for their performing the tasks in the JD. These documents are sometimes called reward schedules.

Not time and motion study results. A JD is not a time and motion study write-up. Time and motion studies are done to identify better means of performing duties and to set precise cycle time standards for executing repetitive tasks. Time and motion study data are generally too detailed for incorporation in the JD. The JD specifies responsibilities and tasks, not individual motions, and indicates approximately what percentage of one's annual work time is spent on given tasks and responsibilities rather than precise cycle times.

Not a statement of why, or of rationale. The JD's emphasis is not on explanation of *why* tasks are performed. The JD may state overall job rationale and the objectives of certain tasks, but elaborate developments of why is not the purpose of the JD. Separate documents should be written for such purposes. The JD states *what*.

Not a job factor sheet. See Appendix O for a job factor sheet. These are used in job evaluation to rate jobs on their relative value to the organization so that equitable pay—base pay—can be established. Job descriptions can aid in the preparation of a job factor sheet and are used to help score jobs after the factor sheet is established. But job descriptions must be clearly distinguished from factor sheets.

Not a commentary on job design quality. Finally, a JD is not a judgmental document or a commentary on the quality of a job's design. It states only what that design is. Whether it is good or bad must be left to the analyst with an interest in improving the design of the work. See Appendix G for itemization of the kinds of factors that might be assessed when analyzing the quality of the design of work.

WHY JOB DESCRIPTIONS ARE SO IMPORTANT

JDs are highly valuable to the management of organizations for a number of key general reasons:

They describe basic building blocks. JDs are such vital documents because they are models of the basic building blocks of organizations—jobs. All jobs in an organization are interdependent; each job is part of a total system. Significant flaws in the design of just one job can cause a crumbling of the entire organization just as one failing component in a rocket can cause the entire rocket to be unsuccessful in flight. Any system is only as good as its weakest link.

To assure no weak links in the organization, each job must be carefully designed and integrated with others. Preparation and analysis of JDs help assure jobs are well designed and that the parts of the organization pull together for the good of the total system. When employees are left alone without job definition, self-interests will dominate their organizational behavior. Running the organization without quality JDs becomes analogous to building a skyscraper on a pile of loose rocks. The JD is the central tool for guiding an integrated work design effort.

They describe a basic determinant of performance and satisfaction. JDs are highly important because they show how work is designed, and work design is a primary determinant of employee-job performance and of employee satisfaction. Job design affects performance both directly and indirectly. If, for example, work is not laid out for efficient performance, the design has a direct negative impact on performance. If the nature of the work is excessively ambiguous, for example, it has an indirect negative impact on performance by affecting adversely the worker's motivation to work. If the nature of the work is too mundane, it negatively impacts on satisfaction.

Since job designs are such a powerful force affecting performance and satisfaction, they must be carefully engineered and constantly monitored. This is where the JD comes in. As a work blueprint, it facilitates efficient job design and analysis of that design for possible sources of performance and satisfaction deficiency.

They give direction. The JD is so useful because it points the way. It gives validity to employee efforts. It assures the worthwhileness of efforts. It gives the employee direction. The alternative is aimless wandering, chaos, inefficiency, randomness, unpredictability of behavior, instability of the organization, lack of continuity of activity from one time frame to the next, breakdown, and mistake.

They are a business prophylactic. As more than one astute manager has suggested, a properly prepared JD is a business prophylactic. It serves as a safety net. It helps prevent scores of nasty problems from emerging. It helps prevent employee grumbling. It helps keep regulatory agencies in check. It helps fight lawsuits related to employment practices. The list is lengthy.

The JD confirms that work has been planned, and when an organization's work is planned there is a much higher probability of organizational success than when things are left to chance—seat-of-the-pants—operation and resultant crisis management. Without JDs there is an absence of definition. This means that employee motivation, training, staffing, and performance control are not really possible—indeed, *management* is not really possible.

They justify human resource investment. The JD is so highly essential to successful organization life because it represents justification for the organization's investment in typically the most expensive of all organizational resources—the human resource. JDs show how labor's energies are to be spent. They help prove the need for the human resource and help give top management a degree of control over its human resource investment.

They are useful in all phases of human resource administration. The JD is management's most powerful tool because it has so many specific uses. It is an aid in every phase of human resource administration. It is the base document for an entire management system. All components of an organization's human resource management system must be built around JDs. Without JDs, planning and control of the usage of the organization's most costly and valuable resource is assuredly a suboptimal process. Chapter 2 will identify 132 specific uses for the JD in human resource management.

CHAPTER 2

One Hundred Thirty-Two Major Management Uses for the Job Description

In this chapter 132 specific management uses for the JD are presented and briefly discussed. This compilation is not exhaustive, however; JD utility is almost boundless. As one begins to use JDs in various ways one soon discovers other uses for them. Using them in these other ways then leads to even more ideas about how to use JDs. And so it goes.

The purpose of this chapter is to give the reader a broad sampling of JD usages to build understanding of how to use them and to build appreciation for their power as a management tool. It is hoped that the ensuing discussion will stimulate considerable thought about additional uses for the JD. Few other managerial tools come close in variety of applications.

The JD is basically a communications tool. If it is well prepared, it will tell a great deal about a job. This information can be used in every phase of human resource management and beyond. It helps the workers, their fellow workers, their bosses, higher-ups, and people outside the organization. If prepared properly, the JD provides these people with a coherent, concise, comprehensive, and accurate picture of the employee's work world. It can be of tremendous help to management in making decisions relative to possible changes in that work world. This chapter will present an extensive inventory of JD utilities.

JOB AND ORGANIZATION DESIGN

As suggested earlier, job descriptions are to work as blueprints are to physical structures and electrical systems. Can you imagine building a skyscraper, wiring a rocket, or even assembling a bicycle without blueprints? It is similarly impossible to construct or design a job or organization effectively without job descriptions. There are a great variety of specific uses in this area of job and organization design.

For planning work. The JD is a work planning tool. Its preparation helps assure that work evolves from a rational, conscious process. Planned work will do more for the organization and cost the organization less than unplanned work or work that emerges spontaneously. Planned work guides employees toward the interests of the organization rather than toward self-interest. By thinking through the design of a job in the preparation of a JD, work design problems can be anticipated prior to occurrence. The alternative to planned work is irrelevant work, chaotic endeavor, inefficiency, and mistakes. The JD is at the heart of managing work in that it is a plan for doing the work.

For projecting the implications of job change. The JD serves as a model of the work to be done. As a model it depicts key job components and component relationships. It shows, on paper, the *structure* of work. This representation on paper aids in understanding the total job and, therefore, in manipulating the components of the job to obtain different desired results. The model can be "tinkered with" and outcomes predicted prior to any actual job change. Studying a number of JDs associated with a contemplated work system change can give insight into rational repartitionings and reassignments of work, and can lead to an orderly, disciplined transition. Experimenting with change on paper first results in potential problems being identified and addressed before they actually materialize. The JD thus facilitates job change efforts rather than, as so many critics complain, constrains them. A model need never restrict design change. It should only aid in making the results of design change more predictable and the process of design change less costly.

For balancing employee work loads. By comparing the JDs of different employees, the manager can gain insight into how the volume of work, the variety of work, the intensity of effort required, and so on, differs from one employee to the next. Once these things are understood, action can be taken to reallocate or redistribute tasks to better equate work loads. Doing such helps minimize bottlenecks, excessive idle time, and unfairness in the system. Tasks may be taken from the overburdened and given to the underburdened; certain tasks may be shared; some additional (new) tasks may be assigned the underburdened; perhaps employees who are overburdened can have some of their tasks simplified, combined with others, or outright eliminated. The JDs of different employees laid out before you help you discern the proper division of work and the proper distribution of tasks and responsibilities across multiple employees.

For identifying where work simplification and time studies can pay off. A properly prepared JD will indicate the approximate percentage of time each task/ responsibility takes. By picking out high time-consuming tasks for careful study as to ways to streamline, additional productive capacity can be developed and operations' costs reduced. If a certain responsibility requires a relatively great amount of the worker's time, this is where the focus should be for any attempts to make operations more efficient. It does not make sense to invest heavily in reengineering tasks that already absorb a small or negligible amount of time. The opportunity for gain with such tasks is relatively minuscule.

For determining how to group jobs or to departmentalize an organization. JDs may show that different jobs are significantly similar in some respect. Such jobs may be grouped together and the people performing these jobs can then be supervised as one unit (department/division) within the organization. For example, if a number of jobs show functional similarity, the occupants of those jobs may be efficiently supervised by one manager who has expertise in that function. Or, if jobs show marked similarity by physical location, it may make sense to have one supervisor for the incumbents in that location. Or, if the JDs for a number of positions show a relationship to a given type of product, it may be wise to group these jobs together administratively under a manager for that product.

Often, in practice, administrative units are defined first and jobs then carved out from within these units. However, as indicated here, it may be worthwhile to design the *jobs* first and then establish administrative units. There are many ways in which certain jobs may be similar and, therefore, many ways that jobs might be grouped. JDs allow management to depict precisely relevant similarities and alternative modes for grouping.

For determining proper spans of control. If the JDs in a manager's domain show that jobs are significantly different from each other, it is likely the number of jobs the manager should supervise is relatively small. If, on the other hand, JDs show jobs to be considerably alike—similar kinds of work requiring similar skills—it is likely the manager should supervise many of them.

Also, by studying JDs, a determination of the complexity of work can be made. If the jobs in a given domain are highly complex, such as electrical engineering jobs, it is prudent to have relatively few jobholders under a given supervisor. If, however, all jobs are routine, involving just a few, highly repetitive tasks, one manager can supervise many employees. JDs can give thorough insight into just how large managers' spans of control should be.

For discovering opportunities for improving intrinsic work design. By studying a JD one can learn about the appropriateness of such job dimensions as task variety, work cycle length, and task depth. Other intrinsic dimensions of a job such as the task mix (task integration, functional similarity of tasks, operative/supervisory mix, etc.), task complexity/difficulty, the amount of task uncertainty, the degree of job autonomy, the degree of authority attached to the position, the degree of task identity and significance, task sequencing, the rate of task set change, the volume of work, and the degree of task challenge can also be discerned by careful scrutiny of the JD. Recommendations for intrinsic design change that will allow the employee to execute at a higher level of proficiency can be made after analysis of the job with the JD.

For discovering opportunities for improving extrinsic work design. A well-developed JD describes what the physical and social contexts of the job are like. By studying these environments with the help of the JD, one can spot ways to make the physical setting more conducive to performance through such means as temperature and humidity adjustment, noise control, lighting change, and so on. Various insights into factors associated with the social environment that affect performance—such as the frequency with which the worker interacts with others, the number of other employees with which the worker interacts, the physical proximity of other employees to the worker, the kinds of work issues requiring multiple employee involvement—are also gained by analysis of the JD. Analysis of these factors with the JD is the starting point for developing strategies for productivity improvement through control of the worker's environment.

For suggesting areas needing standard operating procedures and methods manuals. By analyzing JDs one can determine tasks that are complicated, time-consuming, repetitive, or, perhaps, common to a number of employees. When such tasks are also tasks that must be performed with minimal error and must yield uniform output, it is useful to develop precise, detailed procedures and methods to assure standardized execution of the best possible means of accomplishment. Once developed, such procedures/methods should be published in a manual for all workers to follow. The JD points the way to where investment in procedures/methods design, and publication of that design, is worthwhile.

For guiding reorganization during organization retrenchment, expansion or improvement efforts. The JDs for positions that are to be eliminated in retrenchment will reveal vital task/responsibility areas that must be combined with other tasks elsewhere in the organization or reassigned to others. The JDs for positions not scheduled for retrenchment will reveal opportunities for absorption of tasks from retrenched positions. Studying the set of all JDs associated, in one way or another, with retrenchment helps management make rational reallocations and repartitionings of tasks. Similarly, during organizational expansion it may make sense to alter present jobs as well as to create new jobs. Review of all job descriptions related to the change will help management decide the best kinds of adjustments to make.

During attempts to reengineer work systems, JDs will suggest what to look at for possible task eliminations, additions, combinations, resequencings, and so forth. Jobs shown to be similar in certain respects by their JDs may all be reengineered as a unit—making the same changes across all jobs in the unit. This can help speed and make more efficient the job change effort.

For helping determine the proper physical location for jobs. A quality JD should reveal how the job relates to other jobs—where job inputs come from and where job outputs go. It should reveal something about the nature and frequency of incumbent interaction with other employees. If a job requires a high level of face-to-face contact with a person on another job, then consideration should be given to locating the two jobs in close physical proximity. Office location, work station location, and general work layout decisions, related to work station spacing and sequencing, can be significantly aided by analysis of job interfaces as depicted in the JD. By studying, with JDs, the nature of employee interaction, management can learn about where to position jobs physically to facilitate both material and information flows.

For determining the number of observations required for work sampling studies. In some companies periodic task time studies are done. To provide statistical validity, an adequate number of task observations must be made. To determine the adequate number, a set of trial observations must first be made. Rather than spend time on a trial set of observations to establish approximate percentages of the time the worker spends on various job elements (tasks), percentages can be pulled from a time-distributed JD such as the one in Appendix A. Deriving an adequate number of trial observations for a job with a large number of tasks could demand a considerable investment of time on the part of the analyst. A properly developed JD, however, provides the needed data at a quick glance.

For avoiding duplication of effort, territorial infringement, and task neglect. If work is left to evolve apart from rigorous written plans, job overlap often becomes a problem. Different workers come to perform the same kinds of tasks or to exercise authority in the same areas. This duplication and infringement is wasteful and creates job conflict. JDs can clearly delineate and separate the responsibilities and authority domains of different workers.

Also by developing JDs, management helps assure *all* necessary tasks are incorporated in the design of work and appropriately assigned. Key tasks are not so easily overlooked if a conscious design effort precedes execution. The chance that critical tasks will be neglected or forgotten is reduced when the JD guides the design effort.

For spotting labor pooling opportunities. Looking at JDs will allow one to identify similar jobs and, thus, employees with similar interests, skills, time constraints, physical work locations, and such. JDs will suggest who might be drawn to serve in permanent or temporary labor pools. In pools, all workers work together processing a particular category of tasks. The employees distribute tasks among themselves such that work loads are generally balanced and such that given tasks are allocated to those best qualified to do them. If it is discovered from JDs, for example, that a number of secretaries in the organization perform essentially the same kinds of duties, it may be wise to move these secretaries into one physical space to process the work of many different managers. With a pooled rather than departmented arrangement, fewer employees will actually be required to get out a given volume of work.

For guiding development of other work-related plans. The goals or objectives one works toward should be relevant and that means tied to a properly prepared JD. Worker objectives should be formulated for each responsibility in the JD. Objectives will not be valid if derived apart from one's prescribed set of responsibilities.

Work schedules—when to do what, how often to take breaks, and so on—can also be improved through study of the JD. For example, if a job requires (as determined from the JD) long-term, strenuous execution of a task, a considerable number of properly spaced work breaks should be built into the job. Or, if certain high-priority tasks (high priority as noted by the importance indexes attached to them) are performed daily, these tasks should be planned for execution early in the day—to make sure they do, in fact, get done and to assure they get done while the worker is sharp. Further, one may determine that the nature of the work as depicted by the JD may lend itself to alternative work schedules such as flextime or 4/40 work weeks.

For studying the efficiency of job design. Using the JD for improving the intrinsic design of work was mentioned above (see "For discovering opportunities for improving intrinsic work design"), but the emphasis there was on design changes that might improve the employee's *execution* of the work. An employee may execute very well but still fall short on performance because the job is not designed *efficiently*—not designed to permit high performance even though the worker has high skill and motivation. By analyzing such elements as the variety of tasks, the time allocated to various tasks, the frequency of task performance, and where various tasks must be performed, the analyst can gain insight into how efficiently the work is set up. Too great a task variety can mean that employees jump from task to task, spending most of their time on task start-up and shutdown. Tasks that must be performed in a number of different locations physically separated by great distance likewise cause performance problems. Too much time (and money) is spent in unproductive travel. Potential production bottlenecks, delays, and sources of error in production can all be isolated by scrutinizing task time allocations, task frequencies, and other information depicted in the JD.

For vertical and horizontal job clustering. JDs can be used to develop families of jobs, which may consist of jobs that range from the simple to the complex in a logical progression in a particular field. Job families of this type constitute a path for the employee to pursue in career advancement. Such a vertical job cluster specifies a career design rather than a single job design. It suggests a series of jobs for the employee to progress through. Each successive job demands a higher level of skill, knowledge, and commitment than the previous.

Horizontal clusters can also be developed. Such clusters specify lateral transfer opportunities for employees—a number of different jobs, at essentially the same administrative level in the organization, through which the employee can move with relative ease and a minimum of cross training. Horizontal clusters are often important to help indicate where to move a worker if the company wishes to make room for a new up-and-coming star.

For analyzing job specificity versus ambiguity. Some jobs can best—perhaps only—be described with very general task statements. Precisely what one does on the job is uncertain or so different from one execution to the next that it does not make sense to pinpoint fully the details of all that may go on in the job. Other jobs encompass very specific, stable, definable kinds of tasks and routines that are amenable to precise, written disclosure. With high job specificity, or definitiveness of content, efficiency of execution can usually be maximized, employee performance can be accurately measured, and, because employee behavior expectations are clear, a higher level of employee motivation can often be derived. With ambiguous jobs there is, among other things, opportunity for the employee to engage in behavior not completely compatible with organizational aims. But this behavior tends to be more of an expression of personality and is, therefore, self-satisfying. Understanding degrees of specificity and ambiguity aids decision making in many areas such as what style of leadership to use with the employee and what kind of performance controls to use.

For determining the kind of authority to attach to a job. Authority must be commensurate with responsibility. That is, one needs rights to command others, make decisions, and commit organizational resources that are sufficient to get the job done efficiently. By analyzing the tasks one is responsible for, management can gain insight into what line, functional, and staff authorities the incumbent ought to be able to exercise. Authority is a dimension of job design and the authority attached to a position should be indicated in the JD; but decisions about this authority of the position can usually be better made by careful analysis of the responsibilities of the position first.

For assessing the randomness of demands on the worker. Knowing the unpredictability of requirements made of the employee can help in understanding and troubleshooting sources of such things as employee stress, bottlenecks in production, and causes of employee idle time. If, as indicated in the JD, a large percentage of a person's time is spent doing "other duties as assigned" or in performing tasks related to non-controllable inputs of information and materials—inputs from external points of generation—that person may experience excessive work loading during some periods of time and loading that requires far less than capacity effort during other periods of time. Analysis of the randomness of demands can help determine whether or not employees may need help from time to time and whether or not they will be available to help others on occasions.

If it is discovered that work loads often pile up due to sudden input surges, this alerts management to provide buffer zones for the worker. These may be physical spaces, computer memories, or the like, which can store input while it awaits processing. Because the JD sheds light on task demand fluctuation and uncertainty, it helps management avoid some potentially high-cost situations that can result from non-deterministic conditions.

For isolating design strategies that promote health and safety. The fully developed JD tells what, where, in what environments, and under what conditions tasks are performed. It therefore yields insight into possible psychological and physical hazards. If, for example, an employee is responsible for dealing with other employees' gripes 70 percent of each workday, we might expect this employee's psychological health to deteriorate over the long run. Knowing this, action can be taken to provide carefully spaced work breaks or changes of pace to relieve the employee of stress buildup. Similarly, if an employee is found from analysis of the JD to be working in toxic fumes a high percentage of the time, the organization might want to provide additional safety equipment to filter the air or to alter the employee's time per exposure by having the employee frequently rotate to other tasks to get a break. Also from studying work loads and the amount of task repetition indicated by the JD, the employee's needs for physical rest time can be identified and proper work breaks planned to provide periodic rejuvenation.

For guiding the allocation of unanticipated work demands and temporary assignments. JDs show essentially the planned, routine work loads on workers. When unusual, unexpected, or one-shot new assignments come along they should be allocated such that task integration and work load balance are maintained. Scrutinizing the JDs in his or her area allows the manager to pinpoint what positions are best suited for receiving these new or additional tasks.

For determining job input. The JD highlights responsibilities and tasks. However, to execute responsibilities and tasks, workers need informational and material resources or inputs. Properly written duty statements in the JD with attached priorities can suggest to management the kinds and volumes of inputs that must be readied for the worker, as well as input quality and timing requirements. Specifying job inputs may be conceptualized as part of job design and inputs may be written into the JD. But if this is not done, the tasks spelled out in the JD will aid in identifying needed inputs. In any event, spelling out tasks first helps define inputs later.

For guiding the designs of "new" jobs and the writing of JDs for those jobs. By looking at the already well-prepared JDs managers can identify critical types of elements that must be considered in the design of any new position. They need not reinvent the wheel each time the organization needs to prepare a new job. Neither do managers need to struggle with the writing of JDs for new positions if quality JDs already exist for other positions. Already prepared JDs need only be referred to, to discern appropriate structure, style, wording, and type of content.

For determining the appropriateness of task time distributions. One analyzing a job's design must ask the questions: "Is the amount of time spent on each task commensurate with its relative importance?" or "Are workers spending too much time on low-priority tasks and not enough on high-priority tasks?" The JD gives the analyst a quick picture of how responsibility priorities and times line up and thus gives insight into certain changes that may be in order.

For facilitating decentralization. A great utility for JDs is that they clearly define roles. They reduce role ambiguity and, therefore, the amount of daily management attention required to define, communicate, and control organizational activity. Because of this, JDs allow managers to service relatively large spans of control. With large spans of control, fewer managers and levels are necessary in an organizational system. Moreover, flatter systems with fewer managers mean that a higher degree of organizational decentralization will likely emerge.

REWARD SYSTEM DESIGN
AND EMPLOYEE MOTIVATION

The rewards you will want your employees to experience will necessarily depend greatly on the nature of the work they do. Since the job description portrays the job design—the nature of the work—it is highly useful as a base document for guiding preparation of a system of appropriate rewards. There are a great variety of specific uses for the JD in the area of reward system design and employee motivation:

For determining proper pay levels. The base salaries and wages you pay employees should, at least in part, depend on the demands the jobs place on those employees. Complicated jobs requiring much training and experience should pay more than simplistic, routine jobs. Hazardous, high-health-risk jobs should pay more than safe jobs. Jobs high in formal authority should pay more than jobs containing less authority. And so it goes. By comparing JDs and classifying jobs according to the demands they place on workers, pay differentials among jobs can be more equitably established. Formal job evaluation techniques can be used to reflect the worth of the work. Knowing the worth of the job to the company allows you to set wages and salaries that are fair and to respond properly to employee requests for pay adjustments.

For tailoring benefits. Studying the JD for a job will allow management to gain insight into the kinds of benefits that should go to the person doing the job. For example, a job that places high levels of stress on the worker, perhaps because of its inherent ambiguity or because of extreme fluctuations in the demands placed on the worker, should probably be accompanied by a benefits package heavy on time off—vacation time. Or, if a job requires the worker to be immobile for extended periods of time, gymnasium facilities might well be provided to allow for physical fitness maintenance. The JD helps determine what kinds of benefits might be most appropriate.

For determining job dimensions amenable to the development of contingent rewards. Part of every reward package should be a performance contingent component. By reviewing the JD, the analyst can spot those task dimensions for which clearly measurable performance criteria can be developed. Objective measurement of performance along all task dimensions is usually not possible or practical but the tasks that do lend themselves to performance measurement can be selected out and a contingent reward system can be built around these. Task time percentages in the JD will give the analyst insight into what percentage of the work can be put on a reward-for-performance basis. This will help determine how large the rewards should be. Specifying task priorities in the JD further helps the manager determine how large to make performance-based rewards along the different task dimensions.

For motivating by making job expectations clear. The job description can be referred to when there are questions about what the job involves. It tells workers what the organization expects of them. Duty statements give direction *and*, through priorities and time percentages, the JD indicates the magnitude of effort required for successful performance in various areas. When employees know what is expected, they tend to feel the efforts they exert will pay off—will result in achievement. This is motivation. When people feel that effort will be worthwhile, they are likely to exert that effort (be motivated).

The JD inspires employee commitment. The JD demonstrates to employees that the organization understands the nature and value of their role in the organization. Simple existence of the JD gives the job meaning. Also, when employees have JDs to follow they tend to feel more secure because they more vividly see *how* the organization needs them. Further, JDs help employees avoid missing or forgetting about tasks. Morale is boosted by reducing employee uncertainty about what is expected.

For analyzing a job's potential for providing intrinsic satisfactions. This item was discussed earlier, under job and organization design, but should be mentioned again here to highlight just how the JD helps in the context of reward system design. The JD will alert the analyst to such variables as the degree of task depth, the amount of task challenge, the diversity of skill levels required, learning and growth opportunities at work, opportunities to exercise creativity through work, task wholeness, task meaningfulness, task variety, and so on. All these variables can significantly affect worker satisfaction with employment. By studying an employee's JD, a manager can spot ways to enhance worker satisfaction through altering one or more of these factors.

For analyzing a job's potential for providing physical comfort and social satisfaction. This item was also alluded to earlier but emphasis should be given here to the role the JD plays in helping adjust rewards provided by the environment. By studying a JD one can gain knowledge about the social and physical contexts of a job. Task statements, statements about administrative relations, and explicit descriptions of the physical and social environments of the job are among the data that indicate the variety and depth of social relations that the incumbent encounters and the kinds of physical surroundings within which he or she functions. For example, if the job requires that the worker perform a considerable amount of work within a group or small team setting, the JD should indicate this. Such information suggests a great deal about the social satisfactions likely to be derived from the work experience itself. If a job is performed in a comfortable, well-decorated room with soft music playing, the JD should indicate this. Such data tell the analyst that a significant part of the rewards on this job are provided by the physical surroundings.

For helping management recognize when the employee goes beyond the call of duty. Employees often take on assignments, either self-initiated or requested, that go beyond the requirements of the job—beyond what they were hired to do. This happens as employees grow in their positions and become able to contribute positively to the organization in ways not specified by the JDs. By reviewing the JD and comparing its demands with the extra accomplishments of the worker, management has a sound basis for providing recognition for outstanding contribution.

For preparing employees for advancement. JDs for higher level positions tell employees (at lower levels) what they must learn and become proficient at in order to do quality work upon promotion. By studying the JD for a position into which one has a chance to be promoted, one can establish skill development goals that are meaningful and begin working to develop needed skills prior to promotion. Doing this will increase one's chances of being promoted.

For disciplining employees. JDs define work requirements. They are useful for boss and subordinate to refer to during counseling sessions when the subordinate is being reprimanded for non-execution or poor execution of agreed-to assignments. The JD gives the manager support in attempting to convince employees of their (neglected) responsibilities. It provides clear evidence of what types of behavior the organization expects of the employee and, therefore, serves as a standard. Non-compliance can mean the legitimate application of disciplinary measures or penalties (negative rewards). The JD can, for example, help management prove that a discharge from the organization for non-performance of duties is for just cause.

For identifying the potential personal costs associated with high effort. Employees often resist exerting high levels of effort on their jobs because of anticipated high levels of boredom, fatigue, stress, or frustration, associated with high effort. By analyzing the JD one can identify and appreciate those tasks that may be the source of such costs. Once identified, action can be taken to redesign the work to reduce these costs. Better work scheduling, work breaks, better tools, and so forth can be introduced to ease costs. Any such action, in effect, boosts one's willingness to increase energy levels. It increases motivation.

For clustering jobs to be included in a quality of work life program. Through analysis of JDs, jobs that are similar in their psychological and/or physical impact on workers can be identified and grouped together. All jobs in such a group can be treated somewhat identically during an organization's efforts to improve the quality of work life (QWL). Any organization attempting to upgrade the QWL can make its efforts more efficient and, indeed, can more validly assess the results of its efforts by operating on a number of jobs simultaneously. By applying the same QWL improvement strategies to a number of jobs rather than singling out different jobs for different treatment, management also avoids those charges of unfair or preferential treatment.

For helping the employee properly distribute effort. By studying the time percentages and priorities attached to tasks, incumbents can learn how they should use the hours in the day. They can see how they ought to divide their time and effort among different tasks. The JD aids motivation by guiding worker allocation of limited energies.

For preventing worker resistance to assignments. The JD makes clear up front what the worker will have to do for the organization—do at least at some point in time. When employees are first hired they are often given limited assignments. They may be assigned only those sets of tasks that urgently need addressing or they may be put to work on only the easier parts of the job. The company may intend to expand the employee's assignment to the whole job, or to shift the person to another part of the job for which he or she was hired, later on. Frequently employees resist these changes because they have become set in the routine they started with. Sometimes they will question whether the new assignment is what they were hired for. JDs handed to the person when first hired will tell the individual what the whole job is like and allow the worker to anticipate a shift down the road. Knowing ahead of time what tasks will be encountered can mentally prepare the worker for the assignment. When the task demand is actually encountered, it does not generate shock, disappointment, anxiety and accompanying low morale and resistance.

For detecting opportunities for the job to be adapted to individual personality. As mentioned earlier, the degree of specificity in job design can be detected by analysis of the JD. If employees' work assignments are relatively ambiguous, this indicates opportunity for them to shape their jobs, to a degree, to fit their unique needs and personal characteristics. When workers can mold work to match their own personalities, they generally are more satisfied with employment.

For clustering jobs to facilitate the administration of rewards. Jobs that are alike in the demands they place on workers can be grouped together. One type of pay/benefits package can then be established to reward incumbents effectively in all jobs in that cluster. Expensive individualized packages need not be developed for each different job (or each different employee) if all are quite similar on critical design dimensions. The cost of designing and administering rewards can thus be reduced.

For comparing internal wages and salaries with external wages and salaries. Job descriptions do not only help determine internal equity in pay as discussed earlier. By comparing wage/salary data, gathered by survey for jobs outside the organization, with the wages/salaries of like jobs within the organization, management can also determine whether or not adjustments may be in order— adjustments needed to boost employee satisfaction and aid the organization in attracting and retaining its labor force.

EMPLOYEE STAFFING

To acquire the right people to work in an organization you need to compare the skills, talents, and capabilities of candidates with the kinds of demands jobs in the organization place on the workers. The JD tells you what you need to look for in candidates. It helps you efficiently and effectively match employee with job. There are a great variety of specific uses for the JD in the area of employee staffing.

For developing person specifications. Person (job) specifications are state-ments about the skills, abilities, knowledge, experience, and education one needs to do the job well. By studying the duties and responsibilities in the JD the analyst can infer what person specs are relevant and what level of each spec is required to meet performance standards. Once relevant person specs have been established, then information about the degrees to which candidates possess these specs can be gathered and assessed relative to the required degrees (lev-els). Candidates can be objectively compared. Also knowing the set of all specs for the organization allows management to assess how well the labor available in a given labor market matches organizational requirements.

For job posting and preparing job ads. A quality job ad should indicate the major responsibilities associated with the position. The JD gives this informa-tion. When an opening comes up in an organization, the JD for that opening can be posted for inspection by other employees who might be interested in apply-ing for the job, and the JD can be consulted by management for preparing job ads or other recruiting literature for newspapers, technical journals, the local employment service, and so on. To assure ad validity, consulting an accurate and up-to-date JD is a must. Only with a valid ad can the organization assure that qualified people apply for the job.

For designing application blanks. For job application blanks to be worthwhile and valid they need to incorporate questions of applicants that relate to the requirements of the job. To determine useful questions about relevant education and experience requirements, consulting the JD is absolutely essential. The JD tells what the employee will have to do for the organization. Application blanks should ask questions of applicants that will give the analyst information on how well the applicants can do what they would be hired to do.

For guiding questioning during candidate interviews. Interviewing is an often-used means of screening candidates but it seldom, in practice, is a very valid exercise. As with application blanks, interviews should focus on relevant questioning—questions designed to find out how well candidates can likely perform tasks for which they are being considered. Interviewers would do well to have at their ready disposal JDs to help them formulate job-relevant ques-tions. Structuring interviews with questions derived from analysis of the JD and questions that probe candidate potential for performing specific tasks tends to result in a much higher success rate in selecting the best candidates for jobs. Also following the JD in the questioning of various candidates tends to stan-dardize the interviewing process across a variety of candidates. This results in more objective comparison of candidates.

For determining needed personality traits. A good JD suggests much about the physical and social environments of the job, the types of intrinsic rewards one will experience on the job, formal authority linkages to other positions, task ambiguity, task randomness, and so on. From analysis of such factors, one can isolate the personality trait profile a person ought to have for maximum per-formance and satisfaction. Whether one should be aggressive or laid back, people oriented or independent, emotional or even tempered can, like skills and knowledge requirements, be inferred from the JD.

For determining the desirability of investment in work samples and in-depth tests. Work samples and various types of physical and mental employment tests can be expensive; they take time to design, administer, and evaluate. Typically work samples cannot be conducted for all tasks in a JD but the JD can be used to identify high-priority tasks and time-consuming tasks for which work sampling and in-depth testing may pay off. Few tests of employee competence are any more valid than the work sample, so management should use it wherever cost is minimal and often, even when the cost is significant, if the task is critical to the job as shown by the JD.

For designing assessment centers. Assessment centers are established to allow for time-extended testing of candidates in a variety of task situations relevant to on-the-job performance. By using the JD as a guide, valid experiences for candidates can be established and measurement of performance in the center will be a valid indicator of actual job performance after the candidate is hired. The JD allows for building a center that is a good simulation of the real job.

For promoting self-screening by candidates. Not only should organizations attempt to compare candidates for a job, but also candidates should have an opportunity to assess their own compatibility with the organization. Hiring is a two-way process with the organization choosing a candidate *and* the candidate of choice selecting the organization. Often candidates themselves will discover that a good match between them and the organization is *not* possible. Or they may find that a quality match *is* highly probable even when the organization does not sense this. Candidate insight into the quality of the match is fostered by handing candidates JDs to study. This helps stimulate candidate questions for the prospective employer—questions usually relevant to selection of the right person for the job.

For aiding manpower planning and forecasting. Management should analyze the entire set of JDs in an organization and group them into categories of jobs such that the jobs in each category require workers with similar skills, abilities, knowledge, and traits. Then comparing the needed number of employees in a category with the number of anticipated vacancies in that category during a given time period will give management an idea of the volume of recruits necessary as well as the kinds of sources from which the organization should recruit. Also, classifying jobs in terms of similar requirements (skills, knowledge, etc.), gives the organization insight into the volume of potential internal applicants for given job openings.

For standardizing resume screening. How do you compare resumes that are mailed in a variety of forms, styles, and content? How do you evaluate them objectively? Using the JD to assess the information provided by a resume is one solid means for doing this. In studying resumes, the analyst must look for data that tell how well the candidate can do the job—the tasks outlined in the JD. Irrelevant or non-task-related data can be discarded. Without constant referral to the JD in resume assessment it is easy to be led astray. Resumes often give a lot of impressive data. They seek to dramatize the applicant's case. Guidance provided by a close-at-hand JD helps prevent the analyst from losing touch with the real-world staffing requirement.

For determining the most important person specs. Not only can one infer the desired *kinds* of person specs by studying the tasks in a JD, but one can also discern the relative importance of different specs—that is, how much to weigh different required skills and abilities in the selection process. This determination of relative importance comes from a review of the indexes of task importance and the task time percentages given in the JD. The kinds of abilities needed for high-priority/high-time-consuming tasks are the kinds of abilities that should be weighed most heavily in comparing candidates.

For preventing tasks from getting lost during turnover. A serious problem in organizations that experience high turnover, particularly in management ranks, is lack of continuity of work effort from one incumbent to the next. Too limited a record of the task endeavors of the previous employee is left for the present employee. This extends start-up time and cost, and causes every new person to have to reinvent the wheel—to rediscover the role. Even with fast learners, essential tasks are typically forgotten or neglected. Some things just get lost in the shuffle. Quality JDs provide that all-important record to help prevent such problems. They allow for staffing transitions with minimal disruption and mistakes.

For determining suitability for promotion. Analysis of the JDs of job holders gives tremendous insight into their qualifications for advancement to higher level positions. When the JD of a candidate for an upper echelon slot is carefully compared with the JD for the open slot, significant insight can emerge as to the preparedness of the candidate. Comparing the JDs of a number of internal candidates vying for one available position tells you how relevant their respective experiences are. Relevance of experience is a valid predictor of performance.

For determining temporary help needs and worker "loan" opportunities. A quality JD will indicate changes in the kinds and volumes of demands on the incumbent by month, by season, or by some other span of time. During times when demand on the worker is high, it may be prudent to hire temporary help to aid the worker process that extra load. Similarly, when workers face low ebbs in the volume of work they must process, management may wish to have them absorb other job assignments—to help out elsewhere in the organization. The JD gives the analyst a sense of when work overloads and underloads may have to be addressed through adjustments in the manpower applied.

For developing skills inventories. One can infer from the JDs of incumbents what kinds of skills and talents those incumbents possess. Lists of these persons and their skills and talents can be inventoried. These inventories can be consulted when management is trying to find a person to take on a special assignment or when management wishes to assemble groups of people with certain abilities to work on special committees, task forces, or project groups. By surveying the skills available and identifying who possesses these skills, management can engineer integrated teams with optimal skill/ability profiles.

For helping candidates prepare for the corporate campaign. In some companies, usually at the higher executive levels, corporate campaigns may be used as a method of facilitating employee selection. In the corporate campaign internal candidates competing for a certain position have a chance to develop their platforms and to promote themselves for the position. To help candidates do this and to help assure equal opportunity for all candidates, they can be given copies of the JD for the position for which they are campaigning. Possession of the JD will help candidates develop relevant platforms and suggest to them issues to pursue in promoting their candidacies.

For controlling the quality of the staffing effort. An organization can use JDs to (1) compare what hirees actually do with what the organization intends for them to do; (2) monitor the frequency of JD change, in the organization, to accommodate hiree deficiencies; and (3) analyze the JDs of frequently unfilled positions. Using JDs in these ways gives insight into how well the organization executes the staffing function. If hirees typically engage in work not specified by the JD, it could mean that the people hired are not properly motivated to do specified tasks. If the JDs of hirees are frequently changed to avoid deficiencies of hirees, a question must be raised about the quality of the experiences and training of candidate pools. If positions go frequently unfilled, it may mean that additional new sources of candidates should perhaps be tapped.

For revising jobs to fit available talent. Not always, even with the best of staffing efforts, can a candidate be found who can perform well all assignments as specified in the JD. A job may have to be altered to meet the limitations of the hiree. Perhaps a certain task should be allocated to another position. Perhaps a task from that other position can be shifted to the job of the new hiree. The set of JDs involved allows for study of the options for reassigning tasks. Jobs must never be cast in cement. They must recognize the *actual* character of the *available* human resource.

For helping candidates prepare for interviews, simulations, and assessment centers. Not only does the JD help candidates assess, on their own, their strengths and weaknesses for a position, but it also is valuable for helping candidates learn about the jobs for which they are applying so that they can prepare questions for the interviewer and assemble in advance data that might support their candidacies. Every employer should give JDs to candidates well in advance of interviewing and any in-depth simulations or assessment center-type testing. This helps the candidate pursue a more active and involved role during screening. It helps the company avoid missing important cues about candidate potential.

For justifying the need for additional staff, replacement, or retention of staff. When managers need additional help and request from their superiors authorization to acquire such without first providing *proof* of need, they are doomed to failure. A fully prepared JD for a new position will show exactly what the person is to be hired for. It helps the manager convince higher-ups that useful work will be engaged in by a new person. Of course the manager must actually develop a set of tasks that really cannot be adequately performed by others. Once this is done though, that role must be put on paper and sold to the boss. Without the role on paper the selling is difficult. The same applies for replacement of present employees or for defending the need to retain staff. Upper managers may question the need for certain positions. A well-developed JD can help justify that need.

For guiding the quizzing of references. To standardize and make more valid the results of interviews with candidate references, JDs should be used. When asking references questions, the focus—as with other aspects of staffing—should be on how well applicants can do the job for which they are being considered. The JD suggests the right questions to ask. If every reference is quizzed with the same questions, a data base for objective comparison of candidates will be generated. Often in conversation with references, informal chitchat and non-relevant data exchange dominate. By providing structure for the interview the JD helps avoid missing key issues and being excessively redundant in the questioning process.

For helping develop job rotation programs. Job rotation programs make good sense as long as extensive relearning is not required each time the employee moves to a different job in the cycle—as long as the employee can make good use of his or her best developed talents on each job in the rotation. The JDs for different jobs being proposed for a rotation plan can be studied to identify how compatible the different jobs are and how smoothly transitions across those jobs can be made. Some jobs in a prepared rotation plan may place a particular demand on the workers or require a special ability that the workers being considered for the rotation would not be able to quickly adjust to.

EMPLOYEE TRAINING AND DEVELOPMENT

An organization must assure that its human resource can efficiently and effectively perform the work to which it is assigned. New hirees always need at least some training to properly absorb the nature of their work assignments. Every employee needs training when job assignments are changed. All employees continually need to develop, over time, to assure they are of maximum value to the organization. The JD outlines the task areas in which training may be necessary. There are a great variety of specific uses for the JD in the area of employee training and development:

For inferring training needs. The JD and associated set of person specs make the kinds of training the worker needs self-evident. They clearly spell out those areas in which the worker needs training. Training programs can be set up to address the job demands and skill requirements as specified in these documents. During a training program, JDs aid the trainer in teaching the appropriate material to trainees.

For determining in what areas an investment in training makes the most sense. A JD should identify the high-priority and most time-consuming task dimensions. These are the areas for which employee training is most important and for which training generally has the largest payoff. Spending money to train employees for relatively unimportant tasks that take little time may be wasteful, especially if performance along these dimensions is already at an acceptable level. Management should be leery of supporting high-cost training for tasks rated low in importance or for tasks that do not soak up much of the investment in the human resource.

Management in most organizations will constantly receive requests from various employees to participate in short training programs conducted by outside agencies (or consultants) for employees from a number of different organizations. Decisions have to be made as to the likely benefits of participation in these programs versus the costs. By first assessing the skills to be addressed by these programs and then studying the JD to see the priority and time consumption of tasks requiring these skills, management can make a better judgment about the net value of the proposed training.

For orienting new employees. Every new employee needs a period of time to adapt to the organization—no matter how extensive previous experience and training. To speed this adaptation period, new hirees can be given job descriptions for their positions. These will give the employee quick and valid information about what the job requires. One can use the JD as a ready reference until the work is fully learned. The new hiree can use the JD to study the job and to help in framing questions about the work to pose to the manager. JDs used in orientation help assure that information on all parts of the job is conveyed to the hiree and that key tasks are not neglected.

For team building. Often employees in organizations gravitate toward greater and greater states of isolation and independence with the passage of time. Employees have a natural tendency to build personalized work domains. Coordination and cooperation suffer. But employees should develop sharing and helping behaviors. A person in one position can often provide useful information, a helping hand during physical labor, or whatever to a person in another position. Cooperation, coordination, sharing, and helping are behaviors greatly enhanced when workers know about the roles of fellow workers as well as their own. The JDs of fellow workers can be given to employees so that they can better understand and appreciate demands on fellow workers. This greater sensitivity to what others do shows employees *how* they can help and spurs trust and respect for the other person. This leads to a higher level of integrated and supportive effort—a higher level of teamwork.

For self-development through JD preparation. Perhaps the greatest use of all for the JD lies in the learning that comes from its preparation. Asking employees to analyze their own jobs, and to formulate a detailed profile of what they themselves think should go on in those jobs, gives employees insights and appreciations that cannot be obtained in other ways. At no other time will employees think through so completely the nature and rationale for their work than during self-preparation of the JD. In preparing a JD one will begin to see a host of possible changes that may contribute to greater efficiency, better quality, and a higher level of production. Employees are likely to pose thoughtful questions to their supervisors about what they do and why.

It is a valuable developmental effort for the boss to prepare subordinate JDs too. This should not be left entirely up to the Personnel Department. As the boss works through the JD, he or she will, like the employee, exercise a thoroughness of thought about the job not likely to occur at any other time. The boss will likely see numerous opportunities for job improvement during the process of putting the JD together.

Boss and subordinate may each prepare, independently, separate drafts of the subordinate's JD. Then, when they sit down to discuss and resolve differences in perceptions about the job, a superior final design should emerge. Participative JD preparation gets boss and subordinate thinking on the same wavelength about the job. It breeds a meeting of the minds on job expectations.

For identifying training needs relative to tools and equipment. A quality JD should identify the tools, equipment, and facilities with which the employee works. It should provide the analyst with a good overview of the entire set of tools, equipment, and facilities that the employee needs to be trained to use. Sometimes JDs will explicitly identify tools, equipment, and facilities in separate statements not tied in with task statements. When this is done it is easy to identify tool, equipment, and facility training needs. At other times these kinds of resources may be stated within task statements or simply implied by task statements. In any event, the JD serves as the path to identification.

For preparing a trainer. When an organization hires a trainer to design and execute a training program for a certain group of employees, it must somehow fully acquaint the trainer with the roles played by the trainees, the performance weaknesses of trainees, and possible problems with the job designs that these trainees face. Letting the trainer study the JDs of those who will be trained is a quick and easy way for the trainer to gain insight into the jobs of the trainees. It provides the trainer with a framework for preparing the content of the training program and allows the trainer to conduct truly relevant work-related discussions during training. No training for workers may make more sense than training conducted by one who knows little or nothing about the actual work demands on the trainees.

For orienting and preparing outside consultants. The JD is a valuable tool for the outside consultant hired by an organization to improve organizational functioning through improving the structures and processes that channel employee behavior. The consultant addressing interpersonal processes and team development must be aware of how job designs define the nature and quality of interactions among employees. Consultants must understand the jobs of those employees they are trying to help almost as well as the employees themselves. Thorough study of the JDs followed by probing interviews and observations of job behavior is the best way to gain the required insight quickly.

For quickly preparing substitute workers or temporary help. When workers suddenly quit their jobs or are stricken with illness, replacements have to be found immediately. Many firms do not have the luxury of having ready-trained others to step in. Someone new has to be relied on. To provide a minimal acceptable level of preparation for the substitute, the JD should be consulted. The JD should tell, by indicating task priorities for example, what *must* be attended to by the substitute employee. It will not tell how to do the job but it will tell *what* the sub needs to attend to, or get help doing, and what, in the absence of sufficient time to fulfill all task obligations, may be left for attention later. The JD is an efficient mechanism for rapidly communicating a great deal about the job.

For spotting group training needs. The JDs of employees within an organization will indicate interaction requirements with other employees. JDs will identify exchanges of information and material among positions. They will identify who is involved in given resource flows. They will show a variety of aspects of interfacing among employees. Employees involved in exchanges frequently need to be trained, as a group, relative to interface issues. People who work together must be trained together. If people work independently they can be trained individually but the usual case is for workers to be interdependent. They must be instructed as a team relative to those matters that link them.

For guiding cross training and transfers. Employees in an organization often seek lateral transfer because of changing work interests or possession of a growing body of talent they perceive might better be applied elsewhere. The JDs for other positions sought by employees in transfer can be studied by them. From such study employees can identify their strengths and weaknesses relative to other possible positions and can make intelligent choices as to which positions to shoot for. The JD of another position selected can then be used by the employee to help in self-preparation for the position. The employee may want to enroll in courses provided outside the organization to develop skills that are necessary for the new position. Or the employee may wish to observe, in person, the actual execution of certain tasks performed by a competent person in the type of job to which he or she aspires.

For career identification, constructing job ladders and guiding career development. Jobs at different levels in an organization can be arranged into vertical families that consist of a set of functionally similar jobs connected serially from the relatively simple to the complex. Establishing such families allows workers to identify career paths—paths for job progression. Analysis of the JDs of the jobs in career paths helps workers properly prepare for advancement. The set of JDs that shows the design of the jobs in a family gives workers direction over time. These JDs help eliminate haphazard, trial-and-error, search-and-find type behavior for workers as they move upward through their careers. They make vivid the kinds of training one must pursue to qualify for movement along the job progression path.

For identifying who should participate in a given training program. JDs consisting of like tasks can be clustered together. JDs that require similar types of tasks to be executed indicate those workers needing similar types of training. The employees filling the jobs depicted by the clustered JDs can be identified and then brought together for training as a group. If the organization is to invest in upgrading a certain worker's skills, it may be worthwhile to spend some time to spot other workers with similar skill requirements and to include them in the training. This reduces per person training costs. One-on-one is generally too expensive.

For evaluating the success of training. The JD allows management to see vividly what task behaviors in which the employee should engage and, therefore, aids management in designing ways to measure performance. The true test of the success of a training effort is the degree to which it causes relevant task dimensions to be pursued and the level of performance along these task dimensions to increase. Monitoring worker performance with the JD and a derivative performance level assessment device, before and after a training program, will tell you the quality of the program.

For orienting new supervisors on what their subordinates and bosses do. Perhaps the first thing new supervisors should do is learn what their subordinates and superiors do; effective supervision requires high intraction with these people. Quality interaction with another employee can occur only when you understand and appreciate the nature of the role played by that employee. Supervisors must plan, organize, actuate, and control the performances of their subordinates. This necessitates complete and accurate knowledge of subordinate roles. The JD is the supervisor's best initial guide in acquiring this knowledge. Supervisors must also respond to the initiatives of their bosses and provide help to their bosses. To do this effectively means they must know their bosses' roles. JDs provide the clues to what these roles are like.

For designing specific types of training programs/curricula. Training programs that involve role playing, work simulations, case analyses, and such can be properly established only by building such exercises around the real demands on the worker; the JD tells what those are. For role playing to be relevant and worthwhile, employees ought to play roles that closely relate to their real work worlds. JDs allow the trainer to establish such roles. Similarly the JD tells what kinds of simulations are valid. For example, if the employee is expected to drive a truck on the job, video computer simulations can be used to help the employee improve reaction time. Case analyses, as well, are best when cases approximate the real worlds of work. The JDs of trainees will indicate the kinds of issues cases should cover to be relevant for class discussion. The JDs for a career path can serve as the basis of design for an entire training curriculum that progresses from the elementary to the advanced.

For occupational counseling. Not all hirees will be successful at the jobs for which they are first selected. Organizations make selection mistakes. Sometimes this shows up early; sometimes it may be months or a few years before both employee and organization sense a mismatch *or* that a better opportunity exists within the organization (or outside the organization) for the employee. JDs representing different jobs within the organization may be consulted by the counselor and employee in attempting to spot a better position for the employee. JDs acquired from industry or employment-oriented agencies or associations covering various jobs outside the company can also be reviewed by employee and counselor with the intent of providing direction to the employee in landing a different job elsewhere if release of the employee seems in order.

JDs further aid by providing various agencies and groups outside the organization with vital information for vocational and occupational counseling. State job service agencies, government-funded job training programs, and vocational secondary and postsecondary institutions sometimes rely heavily on data contained in job descriptions acquired from real-world firms.

For helping workers learn to manage their time. On occasion workers will be hard-pressed to find enough time to get all necessary work done. Well-written JDs suggest how long different tasks should take relative to one another. These data can help workers plan their workdays—to budget their time properly to allow for accomplishment of all necessary work in an efficient way. The priorities attached to tasks in JDs will indicate to workers what they should attend to and what might be left to slide until the next day if everything cannot be done. Gaining an understanding of the time demands and priorities of tasks can help the worker learn to allocate time properly across the numerous areas that demand attention.

For identifying employees who could profit from sharing information with and helping one another. A worker may be having a problem with some aspect of work, may be looking for opportunities to upgrade performance, or may have information of use to someone else in the organization. By identifying other workers with similar experiences or training—through analysis of JDs—an employee can find out from whom to search out help or with whom to share information. Clustering similar JDs identifies groups of employees who can profit from one another by helping and sharing.

For determining health and safety training needs. Demands on the psychological and physical well-being of the worker are often explicitly stated in the JD, and if not so stated are usually clearly implied. The JD suggests sources of stress and possible physical harm, such as dangerous equipment, toxic fumes, or extreme temperatures. It serves as a valuable guide to areas in which the worker should be prepared to observe good health and safety practices. The JD indicates just how much attention the worker should give to physical and emotional protection measures. It can impress the worker on the value of learning how to avoid hazards.

For guiding the interventions of boundary spanners. Boundary spanners are employees who vault their own organizational spaces and break into the domains of other workers. They force others to deviate from planned routines. They take problems to others; they request actions of others. For boundary spanners to avoid rejection and to gain others' receptivity to their interventions, they must know about the demands on others and use proper tact and timing when making contacts. By studying the JDs of those with whom they must interact, spanners can come to understand better how their interactions with others can be made successful.

For guiding self-training/development. Employees themselves can use JDs that identify tasks, task times, and task priorities as a guide for self-development activity. The task priorities, in particular, tell workers what they must focus on to assure quality performance on the job.

For helping management trainees prepare for training exercises. Training exercises sometimes are set up to model actual organizational operations. During such exercises management trainees will have tasks to do or decisions to make that are as close as possible to reality. Letting these trainees study the actual JDs of the various positions encompassed by a simulation, prior to involvement in that simulation, can heighten their learning efficiency and make the entire training effort more worthwhile.

For establishing outside training and educational programs. Secondary and postsecondary, public and private education and training programs can be designed to provide more relevant ability/skill development if they are structured with knowledge of real jobs in mind. Using JDs from actual organizations can help institutions assemble more pertinent curricula and hire better qualified instructors. Not bridging the gap between the world of work and academia by this method is not uncommonly at the root of claims that our educational institutions are too removed from pragmatism.

CONTROLLING EMPLOYEE-JOB PERFORMANCE

Effective management of the human resource requires that the organization control the performance of that resource. Control involves monitoring performance, comparing what is observed with a standard, and taking corrective action if the actual results do not conform with the standard. The JD serves management in all phases of this control effort. Basically it guides both manager and subordinate in how to go about developing measures of performance and ways to diagnose sources of deficient performance. There are a great variety of specific uses for the JD in the area of employee-job performance control:

For setting performance criteria and assuring valid performance appraisal. Performance criteria are measures of performance—ways to determine the level of employee performance. Typically there are numerous ways performance along any given task dimension can be measured. In general, when measuring how well one performs a task, you will want to look at the quantity of production, the quality, the timeliness, and the cost of doing the task. To set these criteria, the JD must be consulted to assure that criteria are relevant—that they do relate to task dimensions planned for the worker. Performance criteria must be established for each task dimension or activity category in the JD if a valid overall assessment of employee performance is to be made. The JD promotes objective, unbiased, and comprehensive evaluation of performance. It thereby helps as a quality assurance device.

For establishing strategic point controls. The process of control can be very expensive. Organizations usually cannot afford to monitor all things at all times. They must determine specific areas for focusing control efforts. When it comes to controlling employee-job performance, management must often filter out the priority task dimensions and concentrate on controlling performance along these dimensions. The JD tells which task areas are most important and which consume the largest amount of the employee's time. These are the tasks, the execution of which is critical. It is problems with the execution of these tasks that must receive primary attention.

For establishing weights for performance criteria. To assess one's aggregate performance, performance criteria must be weighted to show along which dimensions performance is highly important and along which dimensions performance is of lesser importance. Once criteria are weighted, the employee's performance scores along various criteria can be multiplied by the respective weights of the criteria and then all results summed to yield a composite performance score. The JD can be most useful in establishing valid performance criteria weights because the JD shows task dimension weights. Criteria associated with highly important tasks should receive relatively high weights. Criteria associated with tasks of lesser importance should be weighted with correspondingly smaller numbers. This approach helps assure that performance evaluation is truly job relevant—that it not only involves assessment of the correct kinds of work but that it also recognizes the relative importance of different kinds of work.

For guiding supervisor and subordinate during performance reviews, counseling sessions, and coaching. Most organizations have their managers sit periodically with subordinates to discuss the latter's performance over the past year or six months. During these review sessions, as well as during more frequent and usually less comprehensive counseling and coaching sessions, manager and subordinate identify areas of strength and weakness in subordinate performance and develop courses of action to resolve any problems. The JD can be invaluable in helping boss and subordinate prepare for the review or counseling/coaching session and in helping them organize discussion during the session. The JD helps keep discussions on track, thus helping assure relevancy of discussion. It also helps alert the manager to the overall demands of the worker, thus contributing to a more rational discussion of performance strengths and weaknesses.

For preventing random and self-serving behaviors. The JD prescribes a pattern for employee activity that, in the thoughtful judgment of those who designed the job, is in the best interest of the organization. Without the JD, employees will have considerable opportunity to use organizational resources in pursuit of their own interests or in the pursuit of goals that are not entirely in line with what the organization desires. Without adequate definition, one's activity can often become trial and error and may degenerate to an inefficient randomness. The JD gives needed structure. It gives clear definition of work. The JD tells what ought to go on in a role. It helps prevent non-relevant behaviors from creeping in to excess and, thereby, causing a significant portion of the investment in the human resource to be wasted. The JD can be viewed as providing constraint on informal behavior and behavior not in the best interest of the organization.

When JDs do not exist or are too loose employees have an opportunity to grab large amounts of informal power. They become highly independent. They can reject new assignments, persuade supervisors of the need for job change, get their budgets increased, and the supervisors have little choice but to go along, since there is a lack of sense of real need in the absence of JDs.

For helping top management control work. Top management should not rely only on its immediate subordinates for management of all things farther down the line. Top managers need, at least on occasion, to observe and to correspond directly with key people lower in the organization. Real control comes from having some redundancy built into the communication channels that keep top management informed.

An extremely useful periodic exercise for top management is to study a broad spectrum of JDs throughout the organization. By doing this top management can see how its human resource dollar is being spent. Nobody is in better position to assess the relative work needs and priorities in various parts of a large organization than its top management. Study of JDs gives top management direct control over what is in fact going on. Without such investigation, an organization can easily run astray. Without JDs work systems get out of control and sight is lost as to what you are getting for your dollar investment in the human resource. Top managers have that necessary overall perspective to judge which jobs are really worthwhile, which are not, and what different or additional types of jobs should perhaps be created to better advance the organization. They need to get involved in influencing job designs by reviewing JDs. Such involvement by top management helps keep control of underlings who thrive on creating irrelevant work systems to further their interests in empire building.

For diagnosing sources of performance deficiency. It was mentioned above that the JD is useful during the performance review. Usually managers and subordinates will commence a diagnostic process during the review to pinpoint causes of any low subordinate performance. The JD might show that a work overload was a contributor to the worker's low performance. It may indicate ambiguity of assignment that could easily cause sub-par performance. It may show linkage with other workers who may have caused a performance breakdown. The JD may suggest scores of factors that might be at the root of a performance problem or be contributing to a performance problem.

For suggesting questions for morale surveys. Morale surveys are often conducted by organizations for the purpose of objectively determining the level of employee satisfaction with employment and of identifying sources of low satisfaction. Satisfaction impacts on performance. For example, low satisfaction can mean high absenteeism, rumor generations, on-the-job drug problems, labor strikes, and more. These things reduce organizational performance. The JD can help the analyst formulate pertinent questions about aspects of employment that may affect satisfaction. It indicates to the analyst what kinds of questions to ask about the nature of the employee's work—questions that will indicate the degree of employee satisfaction with work. For example, the analyst may find upon reviewing a number of JDs that excessive task variety is apparently commonplace in the organization. This suggests that the morale survey incorporate questions on this matter.

For developing the appropriate type and frequency of feedback to workers. Employees need to know how well they are doing their jobs so they can improve if need be, and so they can experience the joys of knowing they are on track when such is the case. The JD can help management decide how often to give feedback on performance of different tasks. For example, a highly important task performed a large percentage of the time indicates a need for extensive feedback. A task that is not performed often and/or that is not too important requires less feedback.

The JD can also help management decide the best kinds of feedback. Complicated tasks may require elaborate written feedback statements. Simple tasks will probably require only simple oral feedback. Tasks that involve interaction with others may suggest the desirability of some form of group discussion that generates feedback for the worker from others associated with the task.

For developing job input controls. Employees do their jobs with inputs, or resources, received from other employees or from sources outside the organization. Informational, material, and monetary-type inputs are common. Employees cannot be successful—no matter how high the quality of their task design—if something is wrong with the inputs received. A quality JD should give insight into the kinds of resources the worker receives and the sources of those resources. It should give enough information about resources so that important ones can be identified and some kind of monitoring of the adequacy of the timing, quality, and quantity of those inputs can be established. Often performance breaks down because of flaws in inputs. Therefore, controls on inputs must be thoroughly planned.

For comparing actual worker engagements with intended. The JD is a standard of what tasks should be engaged in by the employee. It shows planned, intended task behaviors. Management must compare (at least at the end of the review period) what actually goes on with this standard (set at the beginning of the review period). If discrepancy exists the hard question must be asked: "Is what *is* going on what really should be occurring, or is that which actually is occurring irrelevant and off track?" Sometimes such questioning will reveal that times have, in fact, changed and the JD has not been kept up-to-date to reflect the change. In this case it should be altered to catch up. But more often discrepancies between intended and actual will reveal a problem. Perhaps certain activities being engaged in have no real payoff for the organization and other essential activities have been forgotten or are being neglected. Employees sometimes gravitate toward pursuit of trivia in the absence of direction to the contrary because such means success without high investment of time and energy.

For self-assessment of performance. Employees need to assume responsibility themselves in performance control. They need to monitor their own performance and self-correct whenever and wherever such is feasible. The JD tells employees what they need to attend to and at what they must be proficient. It tells employees how their time ought to be distributed and what the relative importance of different task areas is. It is a useful document for the employee to have ready access to and is a document employees should, in fact, pull out of the file periodically to review and study for purposes of comparing actual job behaviors with intended. Sometimes employees lose sight of their total jobs—of the mix of duties they are expected to accomplish. JDs help keep workers in tune.

For providing documentation of task expectations. Managers need to communicate tasks orally to employees but the written record is extremely important too. The written document serves employees as a ready base of reference. They can check it at will to find out formal job expectations. It serves as proof of an assignment and provides an element of stability in what is expected of workers. Task requirements for subordinates are not so likely to change with the wind or be subject to the whims and fancies of every different manager that comes along. Once the acceptable job design is found, its description in writing adds legitimacy, relevancy, and an element of permanency. The JD thus becomes a quality source document for any interested and authorized party to use in researching the nature of the job.

For helping determine the proper investment in contingent rewards. Most companies will want to issue a portion of the employee's rewards on the basis of the quality of the employee's performance. But you have to be careful here. Is top performance on some parts of the job equal to top performance on other parts of the job? Should an employee who performs excellent on task A and medium on task B be rewarded the same bonuses as one who performs excellent on B and medium on A? The answer is *no* if these tasks are weighted differently in the JD. Larger contingent rewards should go to those who do well on the more important tasks. High performance on less important tasks is to be commended but any contingent rewards for this performance must be downsized to reflect the worth of the task to the organization. This principle should apply even to low-cost rewards like praise, too. The most recognition should go to those who do well in high-priority areas.

For facilitating accountability. The JD facilitates quality control by pinpointing what workers are accountable for. It not only tells the manager what to check on in each employee's area of responsibility, it also tells the worker what to report on—what to keep the boss informed about. Accountability is, in part, a reporting obligation. When managers delegate tasks, an accountability relation is automatically established. The JD, with its provision of information on task requirements and task priorities, suggests to the employee what things about the job should be communicated to the supervisor as well as the desired relative frequencies of such communication. The JD helps assure a full measure of accountability—the responsibility for tasks is precisely pinpointed and no key work areas are neglected in the reporting process.

For understanding the magnitude of boss-subordinate communication needs. By studying a JD one can learn about task complexities, task uncertainties, required interactions with others, and so on. Routine, simple jobs require relatively few communications between boss and subordinate. Relatively little attention, therefore, need be given to building elaborate means of information exchange between boss and subordinate. On the other hand, when work is complex and non-routine and the probability of difficulties and problems arising is high, extensive attention may have to be given to building strong boss-subordinate communications. Opportunities for frequent interaction may have to exist and means to assure the accuracy of informational transfer may have to be established.

For helping managers position themselves for performance observations. Managers need to check on subordinate performance. This means reading reports, listening to verbal communications, doing annual performance evaluations, and such. It also means that physical observation may be warranted. Managers can do much better at evaluating their people if from time to time they make direct observations. Some intrusiveness into subordinates' work domains for this purpose is essential to obtain true validity in evaluation and to be able to offer truly worthwhile help to subordinates. The JD can suggest opportunities for the manager to observe. A quality JD shows where different phases of work take place, other people with whom the worker interacts, and the relative amounts of time workers spend on tasks. It can give the supervisor insight into how to go about observing so that key activities can be scrutinized with minimal disruption or generation of ill-will.

For guiding personnel system audits. All organizations periodically need to audit how well they are managing the human resource. How well are they designing work, delivering rewards, staffing, training, and correcting for performance deficiency? JDs can be reviewed for possible changes in job design to better meet reward system, staffing, training, and control requirements or limitations. If performance is constantly low on certain jobs, this suggests there may be problems with the personnel system. It may be found, for example, that performance is low on a particular type of job because of poor staffing that results from faulty person specs—person specs incorrectly inferred from the JD. JDs can guide the audit of the organization's personnel system by helping auditors ask the right questions, schedule interview times, and so on. They give, in concise fashion, a total picture of the *system* of jobs in the organization.

For costing out a job. What is a job costing the organization? The time percentages and task priorities in the JD provide some indication of this. An analyst may find that certain tasks of lesser importance consume large amounts of the worker's time. Time is money and the cost of labor's time generally represents the organization's largest cost. If one or a few tasks of relatively little importance consume a large percentage of the worker's time, then those tasks can be correctly labeled as expensive and perhaps an alternative design or lower cost labor should be found. The JD helps cost control by suggesting where cost-cutting efforts ought to be directed.

For guiding the management of job interfaces. When there is frequent and important contact between, or among, the occupants of different positions, considerable attention may have to be given to problems of coordination and cooperation. Since the JD identifies contacts with other jobs, it alerts management to coordination/cooperation-type problems that may require special attention.

For validating selection tests and performance appraisal forms. The JD helps generate maximum employee performance by helping assure that selection tests and performance evaluation instruments are valid. By checking selection tests for job relevance (do they test skills and knowledge really needed on the job?) and by checking performance appraisal forms for job relevance (do they measure how well the employee does actual job duties?), managers can go far toward getting the right people for jobs and toward getting optimal levels of production from the people hired.

For helping the boss be a better supervisor. This is a good point on which to finish this section because it provides somewhat of a summary. The JD aids performance control because it helps managers remember who is doing what and what they have a right to expect of the worker. It helps prevent losing sight of what people are supposed to do. The JD not only helps the incumbent know his or her job but it also helps the boss know the incumbent's job and thereby helps boss and subordinate have a meeting of the minds on what the subordinate is supposed to be doing in the organization. The JD defines role boundaries and conveys what task expectations exist within those boundaries. It helps the supervisor plan, organize, actuate, and control at a more sophisticated level. It helps management run the system efficiently by directing attention to priority tasks and by helping to distribute tasks logically across individuals and departments. In short, the JD helps the supervisor minimize performance problems because its development forces the supervisor to plan for performance problem avoidance.

OTHER KEY USES

The previously discussed five major categories for JD usage in the area of human resource administration far from exhaust the uses management can make of JDs. Additional applications for job descriptions abound. The following will highlight some of these.

For aiding delegation and easing the communication burden on the supervisor. The JD helps management avoid being a full-time babysitter—avoid constant interference with the employee thus allowing greater freedom for the subordinate. Without JDs managers may have to communicate assignments continually, remind people of assignments, ask for reports, and so forth. JDs can relieve much of this burden for the manager. They can be passed out and discussed with the worker at one point in time during the year—no need for incessantly telling the worker what you want next. The JD clarifies assignments and serves as a ready reference for subordinates wondering what their assignments are. Managers may want to issue orally the same assignments as stated in JDs. That is fine. In such cases the JD simply provides that all-important redundancy in communications that increases the probability that the assignment gets through.

For resolving jurisdictional disputes. Workers may not be sure of the tasks for which they are responsible. They may think somebody else is responsible for certain tasks when, in fact, the tasks are theirs. Or they may think a certain duty is in their realm of responsibility when actually somebody else is supposed to do it. Work domain disputes can arise. The JDs of the parties involved can help resolve such disputes. These JDs should clearly state just which tasks go in which jobs. If they do not contain explicit reference to a given jurisdictional question, they are likely to provide enough relevant information about tasks, authority, and so on to aid significantly in resolving the conflict.

For aiding outplacement and retirement planning. More and more organizations are recognizing retirement planning and outplacement as important benefits for the employee and, indeed, as obligations of the organization. JDs can be kept on file for workers, duplicated, and copies given to workers searching for employment elsewhere. Often a JD can serve as proof to another employer of what skills and knowledge a worker has acquired. It can be used by the out-placed in interviews with other organizations.

Also JDs can help employees plan life after work in the company. They suggest areas of interest and expertise that might be drawn upon in the development of hobbies or social and recreational pursuits upon retirement. They can suggest what kinds of part-time or temporary work activities the person is qualified to pursue.

For helping assure compliance with laws and regulations. Many regulatory agencies and laws tell what can be done and what must not be done in relation to demands placed on the worker or the kinds of tasks/responsibilities required of the worker. Equal Employment Opportunity (EEO) laws require valid performance assessment. Such assessment can only exist, according to EEO guidelines, by building performance assessment around a well-prepared JD, which comes from data derived by a formal job analysis. The Occupational Safety and Health Administration puts outright bans on certain kinds of hazardous duty. JDs can show compliance.

People who come back to work after injury may have to avoid certain duties that were part of their original jobs. Revised JDs can show that the organization has, in fact, altered the job to fit the limitations of the injured worker and to meet workers' compensation requirements. JDs can also provide evidence that the company is observing certain health laws and certain work environment conditions insisted upon by insurance companies. In some industries, such as the health care industry, JDs can demonstrate institutional adherence to industry standards and practices. In short, JDs can spell out how employers are observing laws and other imposed requirements.

For providing an historical perspective. A file of JDs kept over time provides a valuable record of how work and administrative systems in an organization have evolved. By reviewing past arrangements of jobs and internal job structures, the organization can spot what kinds of work and administrative systems have been tried before. Such review helps avoid reinventing the wheel and making the costly mistakes of the past. Review of old JDs can serve to generate fruitful discussion on what kinds of work ought to be engaged in—on the rationale for engaging in certain activities as opposed to others. By reviewing the organization's history, points of continuing weakness as well as strength can be singled out and better understood. Chronic areas of weakness can then be more constructively addressed for correction. Strengths can be more intensely pursued.

For defining group work. JDs are not only worthwhile for individuals; group work should also be consciously designed and defined. Usually within a group, committee, or task force, individual assignments are not spelled out but the overall group should have clearly defined functions and authority. Group JDs can give groups a true sense of why they exist—a clear picture of what the group is supposed to accomplish. As with JDs for individuals, JDs for groups can help in planning rewards for groups, in picking the right people for participation in the groups, for training group members, and for controlling group performance.

For encouraging management to specify temporary assignments in advance. A serious problem in many organizations is the assignment of temporary work to certain employees. Often such work is not compatible with normal assignments, overburdens workers, or agitates and frustrates workers because they are not given opportunity to plan ahead and properly integrate the new assignment into their work routines. Much temporary work *can* be planned ahead, however, and communicated to the worker well in advance. A good practice is to write into JDs, when they are annually reviewed, a temporary assignment section that spells out new responsibilities that are of a year or less in duration. This practice helps assure that the JD is an accurate reflection of the total work design (routine and temporary work) and it gets management to think through needed temporary activities before they actually must be confronted.

For aiding analysis of the organization by outside agencies. Accrediting agencies and regulatory agencies of various types need to inspect organizational operations from time to time. JDs guide these agencies to the appropriate people to talk about matters relevant to their concerns. Some agencies, for example, may insist that certain kinds of activities be performed, that certain employees have a particular set of tasks to perform, or that work loads not exceed such and such a level. Such is common in the medical field and in education. By studying JDs, the outside agency receives insight as to what to investigate as well as with whom to talk.

For providing stability and continuity. JDs are vital in helping organizations cope with rapid job change and organizational realignments. They provide for stability and continuity in the organization. They in no way thwart change as some writers have suggested. Indeed, they facilitate change by helping assure key work elements are not overlooked in the change process and that the process is controlled. Without JDs change may occur for change's sake. Rapid change can mean certain old, but nonetheless important, tasks get lost or neglected as new assignments are engineered into jobs. Chaos and inefficiency become the norms. The preparation and revision of JDs along the way—leading rather than trailing the change effort—assure a measure of forethought and systematization in change not likely achieved by other means. This helps prevent work systems from evolving into higher states of entropy.

For helping employees see the justice in the system. Sometimes employees get disturbed and morale suffers when they think they are not getting paid as much as someone else who does essentially the same type of work, or when they think they are doing more than others but for no more pay. On many occasions such attitudes and feelings are the result of erroneous perceptions that emerge because of excessive secrecy in pay and work assignments. When the organization gets out the JDs for review for those employees who are upset, the bases for being disgruntled more often than not disappear. Workers find the inequities they thought existed do not in fact exist. JDs show employees what others do and allow for objective comparison with what they themselves do.

For understanding the roots of productivity decline. Change alone is not good or bad; but by reviewing how JDs in an organization have changed over time and by looking at how fast they have changed, one can gain insight into why the organization may be experiencing productivity problems. For example, if you discover that given workers' jobs are constantly and radically being altered in content, a legitimate question arises as to whether or not these workers ever develop very high proficiency. Similarly, if you find that workers are continually having to develop new working relations with others, a question arises as to whether or not quality teamwork ever emerges. If change is not paced right and not of the right kind, the human resource finds itself always in an inefficient start-up mode.

For defending against claims or employment discrimination or abuse. Any organization can be called to court in an employment abuse or discrimination case. To defend itself, the company may have to present JDs to demonstrate what job demands and requirements are like. People bringing charges of faulty employment practices usually do so because they have been rejected or denied what they perceive as opportunity afforded others. The JD can help show why such denial or rejection was made. They can help show, for example, why there are pay differences, why certain people were promoted and others not, why certain people were not hired, why certain workers were not accepted for a training program, why one position was retrenched and not some other.

For guiding determination of exempt and non-exempt status. Exempt employees are those to whom the company does not pay overtime wages or salaries. Non-exempt employees must be provided overtime pay in conformance with wage/salary legislation. By reviewing the JD, the analyst can decide which category the job most properly belongs in. Usually supervisory-type work and the work of high-level staff people and professional employees will be classified as exempt. Management will expect them to do the work whenever it needs doing for a fixed wage or salary. Operative employees and perhaps some section leaders, or foremen-types, with relatively little supervisory work will usually be classified as non-exempt. The important point is that the organization be consistent in its classifying of particular jobs. Sometimes grievances arise from employees about their jobs being improperly classified. In such cases review of the JD usually helps explain why the job was so classified or review may indicate to both management and employee that a change in status is, indeed, needed.

For aiding analysis of informal employee groups and coalitions. By studying JDs that specify formal relationships among employees an analyst can gain insight into why certain informal relationships—cliques, power groups, friendship groups—form. JDs can provide information about how strong or cohesive these groups are, how far they permeate the organization, and the possible size of the membership of these groups. This is because JDs show such factors as physical locations of work, communication ties among positions, positions requiring similar employee skills and interests, and such. These planned factors influence the character of unplanned work and social systems that emerge spontaneously within the organization. Knowing about informal groups helps management in such areas as deciding how to use the grapevine for communications, gaining support for plans, and building real interpersonal trust among employees. The JD is a formal work plan but the design it represents shapes much informal organizational behavior.

For aiding in identifying informal leaders. Employees who are centrally located in a physical sense, who have contacts with large numbers of others, who perform highly important work for the organization, who are single links in vital channels of communication, are strategically positioned individuals. They are in natural positions for exerting influence on others. These people, in time, tend to emerge as informal leaders—fully as influential and often more so than those in the organization designated as *formal* leaders or managers. It is important to work closely with informal leaders and to have their support for activities and plans developed by the company. Other employees will follow the informal leaders. The JD helps identify who plays in roles that will foster their emergence as informal leaders.

For guiding the preparation of employee handbooks. Employee handbooks usually provide a body of information about jobs, reward systems, performance evaluation procedures, training systems, staffing issues, and so on. Job descriptions should often be included in them. What is more, JDs will suggest issues related to various aspects of employment that should be discussed and explained in detail in a handbook. Certain work-related policies and rules, work methods and procedures, and safety regulations that are relevant for quality employee performance will be suggested by the JD as areas to cover in the handbook.

For guiding labor and management in collective bargaining. The JD is a written document that can help focus work-related discussions on specific tasks and work arrangements. Both management and union can better judge likely performance/productivity/cost changes coming from proposals for alteration in jobs made by the "other side," if they have JDs readily available during presentation of the proposals. JDs laid out at the bargaining table allow both sides to trace quickly the probable ramifications of proposed changes.

Once agreements on jobs have been reached, final JDs can be prepared and both sides can indicate official mutual understanding and acceptance by signing them. As mentioned earlier, however, JDs must not be viewed in and of themselves as contracts that will remain inflexible for an extended period of time. They are good for helping reach clear agreement for the short run, but should not be regarded as long-term contracts unless they are written in a general enough way to provide for flexibility in worker assignments.

For helping avoid and resolve employment complaints and grievances. There is no limit to the kinds of grievances employees submit over time. Well-prepared JDs are found useful in helping prevent and resolve grievances that arise out of lack of clarity of expectations, grievances related to the failure of others to do their jobs, grievances related to perceived unfair treatment in work assignments or rewards, grievances on evaluation of performance, grievances related to improper staffing, or grievances related to lack of training opportunities. The JD helps management and worker have a meeting of the minds on work-related issues. It helps them view the job in the same way. It is an information source that can provide guidance on how to deal with factors about which the employee finds opportunity to complain.

For bounding behavior and helping management avoid violating union-management agreements. Management may want to alter assignments—add to work loads, change tasks, delete tasks. Management may want to boost the pay of some workers and not others, or provide training to one work group and not others. Management may want to contract with an outside firm to do some specific tasks. Consulting JDs can remind management of previous agreements and of what is fair and not so fair—of what makes sound sense and of what does not. JDs are helpful in constraining management action to a sound and equitable path.

JDs prevent employee abuse by aggressive management by defining the limits within which the organization has decided the employee should operate. Management is discouraged from making arbitrary and excessive demands on the worker. JDs constrain and bound employee behavior to protect the employee and the organization.

For aiding behavioral research related to employee performance, and to job and occupational characteristics. Job descriptions provide a wealth of data of interest to researchers. Researchers can study JDs to develop hypotheses about how particular job structures affect satisfaction and performance. They can study JDs across different organizations to detect patterns of differences and similarities. They can lump like JDs from different organizations together to gain broader insight into general demands in an occupation. There is no end. Well-developed JDs can provide anyone doing research in organizational behavior with a volume of quality data, unmatched by other sources.

For social security administration. The U.S. Social Security Administration uses job data from JDs for a variety of purposes such as compiling statistics on death and injury rates per job type, paycheck deductions per job type per geographical area, pay rate differentials within given organizations, and so on. Usually the organization supplies data desired by the Social Security Administration on forms sent out by the Administration. But the data come from JDs.

For guiding design of organizational communications systems. JDs show contacts and linkages among workers—materials flow linkages, authority linkages, information exchange linkages. By studying aggregations of JDs in an organization, flow patterns—types, densities, fluctuations—can be isolated. These patterns can then be analyzed for the purpose of designing more efficient communication networks throughout the organization. A key point here is that an *aggregation* of JDs, when studied as a whole, can yield entirely unique insights into total work system design and the communication network that must exist to integrate that design.

CHAPTER 3

How to Write a Job Description

The true extent of the usefulness of the JD depends immeasurably on the quality with which it is prepared and the degree to which it fully and accurately depicts the design of the job. JDs must be written clearly. They must cover the right issues and include the right specific bits of information. They need to be properly structured. They need to give an accurate picture of the whole job, which means sufficient detail as well as coverage of all expectations. This chapter will show the reader how to develop a JD that does nearly everything it ought to—a JD that can be used in each of the 132 areas specified in Chapter 2.

Writing quality JDs takes time and costs money; keeping them current is an added burden; but the investment is, without question, worthwhile for most types of organizations. Some organizations may be wise to prepare a simpler JD than what is presented here. If the organization is small and the nature of operations is relatively unchanging, the JD is less useful; but when the organization gets beyond a half dozen or so employees, and faces changing demand, new technologies, and the like, the JD becomes indispensable. When the scope and depth of operations become too large to keep all in your head, the JD is an absolute must.

Job description format and content should, in large measure, depend on the uses to be made of the JD. Therefore, those uses should be clarified *before* efforts are made to prepare JDs. For example, if the JD is to be used heavily for determining management salaries, working conditions, asset accountability, and specific supervisory duties should be spelled out in the JD. If, however, the main purpose of the JD is to provide information to prospective employees, these factors may be left out and greater emphasis put on general operative functions.

The JD format presented in this chapter is generally applicable. It can be adapted to any type or size of organization. It is a format that can easily incorporate adjustments as updating is required. It is not an overly elaborate format. It could include more. It is a workable format—easy to read and concise. If the organization wishes, the format discussed here can easily be simplified while maintaining its greatest strengths.

MAJOR SECTIONS OF THE JOB DESCRIPTION

A well-written job description incorporates a number of major sections. See Appendix A for reference during the following discussion. The sample job description in Appendix A (one drawn from the real world) covers most of the items mentioned below.

Job ID Section

The job description should begin with a job identification section, which includes the title of the job and any identifying code numbers. Job titles, contrary to the opinion of many, are important because if properly stated, they can help considerably to clarify the nature of a role.

The identification section should label the grade level (useful for pay purposes) of the job if such applies, the department and/or division of the organization in which the job exists, the name of the company, the physical location of the job, when the job is executed, the organizational level of the job, exempt or non-exempt status of the job, and any job families or career ladders of which the job is a part. This section should also indicate the date the JD was prepared, who provided input data for it, who wrote it, and who approved it. Signatures of the incumbent and the supervisor should be in evidence to indicate acceptance.

Function Statement

After the identification section an overall function statement or summary statement should be provided, which is like a mission statement for the entire organization. It sums up in a short paragraph the rationale for or the general purpose of the position. The statement attempts to explain *why* the position exists. Such a statement is extremely valuable because it gives the reader of the JD a concise overview, or big-picture view, of the job. It tells the reader what the main thrust of activity in the position is all about.

Often workers get lost in the details of a job and lose sight of their overall function. When this happens one can lose a sense of purpose in the organization and the job may come to lack meaningfulness. Function statements spell out the reason the job is needed and thus help overcome these problems.

Accountabilities

Following the statement of function the JD should state the major results expected from the job. This section is a good follow-up to the function statement because it makes clear the key outcomes expected. This section, usually referred to as the accountabilities section, is not so much a statement of activity or duties but rather of what the incumbent is supposed to accomplish—the *results* of activity. It can aid significantly in evaluating performance, but remember that performance criteria and standards are best left for a separate document—the performance evaluation instrument.

This section may also state what organizational assets the incumbent is charged with protecting and using properly—that is, asset accountability. Sometimes, as in Appendix A, when duty statements are categorized by major responsibilities and written properly, this section might better be placed later on in the JD and focus only on assets without depicting expected results.

Organizational Relations

Next, if not adequately covered in the ID section, the JD should clarify how the job fits into the organization's system of jobs. How does the job relate to others administratively and operationally? A job description should indicate how the job fits into the line structure of the administrative hierarchy—that is, who the boss is and who the subordinates are—and should indicate any functional authority and staff linkages to other positions. A given job can simultaneously have a host of different types of administrative linkages—line authority, staff authority, and functional authority—to other jobs. All these relations should be spelled out to make clear how the position uniquely fits in the administrative system. Typically JDs do not say enough about how jobs are part of the total system. Because of this, making constructive changes in jobs is often a difficult process because the possible repercussions of a given job change cannot easily be traced throughout the organization.

Job descriptions should describe the many *work* (operational) relationships that exist with respect to the job. In reading a JD one should be able to discern what part a given job plays in the total work system—how it interrelates with work performed on other jobs, who else the worker makes contact with, and so on. In the organizational relations portion of the job description, you should show informational, material, and monetary resource flows to the job as well as the sources of these flows. Likewise, the outputs (results) of the job should be reiterated and destinations of these outputs made clear. Again, job change efforts are immensely facilitated by doing this.

Added to the above should be a full description of feedback mechanisms. Job design involves building feedback systems for the workers. These systems keep workers informed about how well they are performing on their jobs. Written reports, word-of-mouth comments from the boss, test results, data from mechanical counters, and information from workers down the line all represent mechanisms for helping employees better understand how well (or poorly) they are doing. Feedback systems frequently tie the workers to other parts of the total work system. When redesign is necessary, a precise picture of this performance control component of job design is vital for tracing the ramifications of change. Finally, in this section, any areas of shared responsibility should be made clear. This can be vital information if performance evaluations are to be valid. It is critical to assure clear accountability and control.

Duty/Responsibility Statements

Following the description of organizational relations, task (duty) and responsibility statements should be identified in a modified list format. This duties/responsibility section is the heart of the JD—a description of the job's intrinsic design. Statements must be written properly and cover all dimensions of the job. More will be said later about how to prepare this section of the JD. Task/responsibility statements tell the reader precisely what the incumbent does for the organization—how the human resource is used and how that resource spends its time.

Independent Authority

Following the section on duties the JD should describe the independent authority of the position. It should be clear just what decisions the incumbent can make on his or her own without clearance or authorization from higher up. The organizational resources—and size of those resources—that the job holder can commit to use should be identified. This section spells out the depth and scope of the incumbent's official authority to get things done. Note that the real-world sample in Appendix A does not include such a section.

Environments

Next in the JD a description of the physical and social contexts in which the tasks are executed should be given. Description of the physical context should call attention to any hazardous conditions, to lighting, sound, temperature, and atmospheric conditions and to visual factors present in the environment such as decor and coloring.

Emotional, mental, and physical demands should be delineated. It is critically important here, if not done elsewhere, to describe the volume of work (a key dimension of job design) expected of the worker. Does the job involve a heavy work load? Or is the work load relatively light? It may be useful to show comparisons with other positions.

Description of the social context should refer to the incumbent's physical proximity to other workers, the frequency of verbal contact the incumbent has with others, and opportunities for non-task, socioemotional interaction with others. The extent to which the job is an integrated element of a team effort and the degree of autonomous control of work exercised by the worker can also be indicated here if not spelled out in previous sections.

Tools, Equipment, Facilities, and Layout

A section depicting the tools, equipment, facilities, and work layout systems confronted by the employee should come after the description of physical and social contexts, if this is not adequately incorporated within duty statements. This section should vividly show the technical environment. It tells the reader what kinds of relatively fixed resources the employee uses to get the job done.

Other Items

Since the purpose of the JD is to show, as clearly and completely as possible, the design of the job, various other bits of information can be added. If the data are useful and are on the design of the job, then add them as long as they are not too costly to gather and as long as they do not contribute to excessive complexity and confusion.

It may be worthwhile to elaborate on the kinds of inputs and outputs associated with the job. Statements about the kind of work system—serial, parallel, departmented, pooled—the job is a part of may be included as well. Sometimes it makes sense to discuss any other jobs with similar characteristics that fall into a family of like jobs—horizontally or vertically.

What the Job Does Not Include

Often it is desirable, in the interest of making the job design clear, to include another section that indicates what tasks/responsibilities are *not* included in the job. For example, sometimes workers become abused when they take instructions from many sources. To prevent this you may want to restrict what workers will be permitted to do by including explicit statements clearly showing forbidden territories. Employees in labor pools often find themselves doing anything and everything that nobody else seems to have time for or that nobody else wants to do. Excessive work loads and worker stresses soon emerge. This is the kind of situation that can be avoided if the JD incorporates statements of tasks in which pool members will *not* engage.

MAJOR PARTS OF THE
DUTIES/RESPONSIBILITIES SECTION

This section should really list all the ways in which the worker is expected to use the workday. It should be a set of activity expectations. Some of these activity expectations are probably not properly classified as duties or responsi-

Figure 1
Categorized Activities

	% of Time	Priority
1. Work activities		
1.1 Planned work		
1.11 Routine work		
1.111 Individual assignments		
1.1111 Supervising responsibilities		
1.1112 Operative responsibilities		
1.11121 Position specific		
1.11122 General		
1.112 Group assignments		
1.12 Temporary work		
1.121 Individual assignments		
1.1211 Supervisory responsibilities		
1.1212 Operative responsibilities		
1.12121 Position specific		
1.12122 General		
1.122 Group assignments		
1.2 Unplanned work		
1.21 Self-initiated activity		
1.22 Directives from others		
1.23 Unexpected problems		
2. Non-work/semi-work activities		
2.1 Delays/idle time		
2.2 Travel		
2.3 Work breaks		
2.4 On-the-job socializing/self-interest pursuit		

bilities but they should be built into the job description to show the true, total design of the job.

A simple listing of activity expectations (obligations) is not sufficient, however, for this section of the JD. Activity obligations should be categorized. Among other things, categorizing makes the intrinsic structure of the job clearer. A full rationale for categorizing (formatting) will be presented later in this chapter. Presented here are some useful ways of categorizing tasks and activities in the JD.

Figure 1 identifies major and a variety of subcategories of activities in which employees might engage. This is a generally applicable framework—applying to any type of job in any type of organization. Specific workers in specific organizations, however, may not engage in some of the categories of activities indicated in the figure.

Work Activities versus Non-work/Semi-work Activities

To really understand what a job is like, it is useful to point out that workers do not spend all of their time working. This point is seldom made in the classical JD, but formatting as in Figure 1 shows much better the *real* design of the job. It shows that a worker engages in non-work, or semi-work, activity (category 2) while employed as well as in work activity (category 1). On-the-job socializing; time spent waiting for information, materials, and tools or for problems to be resolved (delay time); time spent walking or riding to where work is to be done (travel time); plus time taken to rest, get a soda, or visit the restroom can make up a significant portion of one's workday. Not acknowledging this type of activity in the JD misrepresents the true design of the job and the demands on the worker. The classical JD lists only category 1 activities—*work* activities.

Planned versus Unplanned Activity

To further illustrate the true structure of a job, recognition should be given in the JD to *unplanned* work (category 1.2) as well as to planned work. Employees never spend all their time pursuing planned activities. No organization, no matter how expert and competent its managers, can project ahead (plan) all that has to be done. In many organizations, numerous employees spend a high percentage of their time processing the unanticipated, the unexpected, the unforeseen. They do things (indeed, they must do things) that no manager could have listed beforehand in the responsibilities/tasks section of the classical JD.

Most workers, worth their salt, will be innovative and inquiring from time to time and will want to initiate new courses of action for the good of the organization. This is self-initiated—category 1.21. Workers will have to respond to unanticipated directives from management and spur-of-the-moment requests from peers from time to time—category 1.22. Moreover, responding to unexpected problems (category 1.23)—major equipment breaks, a rash of unpredicted worker injuries, and the like—can occupy a great deal of one's workday too. The classical JD, however, does not acknowledge this more-often-than-not major time-consuming category of worker activity and consequently it falsely reflects the true nature of the work. Every JD should include an unplanned work section that is filled in and reviewed at the *end* of each review period.

Routine versus Temporary Activity

Frequently, temporary planned work (category 1.12) is left out of the JD altogether. Here we are referring to planned work of a year or less in duration. Management will want to give most workers some temporary assignments in addition to their full-time, repetitive, year-in and year-out assignments. Such activity should be prepared in writing and added to the rest of the JD (using an attachment if you wish) at the *beginning* of each review period. If it is not, valid evaluation of worker performance during the period is next to impossible. A true picture of the demands on the person holding the job is not given by the JD, which shows only the recurring, ongoing duties.

Acknowledging the necessity of a temporary component in most workers' jobs helps make it clear that annual attention should be given to updating JDs. Too often JDs sit and become outmoded. Getting them out of the file once a year to adjust for temporary work can help spur that so-essential, regular total document review and renovation.

Individual versus Group Activity

Much of a worker's work may be his or her responsibility and his or hers alone, but frequently management will want to give group-level assignments (category 1.112). One may be assigned to a committee, project team, or task force. Specific tasks will not be assigned the individual. Instead the group is given a job to do and specific assignments will likely come from the group leader or from an informal consensus among group members. These group assignments can make up a significant portion of one's job and should be made distinct from individual work assignments because management typically does not exercise the same degree of control over group assignments. End-of-year performance assessment of a group member's work may have to be undertaken in a manner quite different from assessment of individual performance.

Supervisory versus Operative Responsibilities

JDs would do well to separate supervisory responsibilities (category 1.1111) from nonsupervisory responsibilities (category 1.1112). All managers have both. Both categories usually occupy a substantial percentage of the manager's time. Showing how a manager's time is distributed between these two categories tells what the manager's job is really like. Some so-called managers may spend as much as 80 percent of their time on operative (non-managerial) work. Only 20 percent is spent managing. Other managers will spend as little as 20 percent of their time on operative work—or doing, while spending 80 percent of their time on what a manager is paid for—planning, organizing, actuating, and controlling.

Operative and supervisory responsibilities may be further classified to aid in interpreting the structure of work. Tasks/responsibilities that use the same resources may be grouped together. Tasks done in the same work location may be grouped together. Frequently, different tasks must be done at different times of the month or perhaps different tasks are done during different seasons of the year. Categorizing these tasks by *when* they are performed is fairly common. Also categorizing tasks by relationship to products, services, or types of customers served is sometimes used.

Categorizing by Function

Perhaps the most useful way of subdividing operative and supervisory duties is by task similarity. Tasks that are functionally alike or tasks that relate to accomplishment of one large, distinct unit of output may be grouped together. An efficient and relatively simple way to prepare JDs is to break the job into major functions for which the employee bears direct responsibility. These functions should be defined in such a way as to cover essentially all of the tasks incorporated in the job. The JD in Appendix A is so structured. Note that in the sample in Appendix A, major areas of functional responsibility are first defined and then each is broken down further into supervisory and operative duties.

Without a subdividing approach, JDs often ramble on with literally dozens of seemingly unrelated tasks. It becomes difficult to make any sense out of the job. Categorizing by function sharpens the focus of a JD and makes vivid key structural characteristics of the job. Six to fifteen major function groups seem about right for most jobs. This number allows for ease of conceptualization of the job and is generally sufficiently comprehensive.

Position Specific versus General Responsibilities

Finally the JD should distinguish position specific responsibilities (category 1.11121) from general responsibilities (category 1.11122). General responsibilities are those kinds of duties most other employees are held accountable for too. These general responsibilities are responsibilities common to a large cross-section of the work force. Position specific responsibilities are those unique to the specific position being described by the JD. Distinguishing position specific from general responsibilities helps clearly differentiate a given job from other jobs, while at the same time clarifying expectations that are the same for many employees.

Many kinds of general responsibilities are neglected by the typical JD yet are highly necessary for the employee to perform if the organization is to succeed. Following are some examples. A general control responsibility that should be indicated in every manager's JD is the responsibility to do a formal assessment and review of subordinate performance periodically. This is a critical management activity that takes considerable investment of time and effort if done right. All managers should be evaluated on how well they conduct performance evaluations on their people.

Responsibilities for various types of communications such as annual reports on performance to the boss, monthly information to update subordinates, or information on any problems arising should be indicated in job descriptions. JDs often tell what transformation or form utility tasks one has to do but forget to convey the nature of the communication that should surround or accompany these tasks.

The employee's responsibility for semi-annual or annual self-evaluation of performance and for preparing for the follow-up performance review should be indicated in the JD. Every employee should be charged with the responsibility of providing evidence of performance. This is accountability. If we expect employees to be accountable, we should not hide this expectation. It ought to be spelled out in the JD. This is a highly important employee responsibility and how well the employee does this should be a consideration in the evaluation of the employee's performance.

Employees should also be charged with the responsibility for annually updating their JDs. Of course, employees' efforts here would not be the only source of information for updating but certainly it would be one important input. Again, how well employees do this is a dimension of their performance that should be evaluated and, therefore, should be evidenced in the JD.

Other general responsibilities that may be indicated in the JD (instead of hidden elsewhere in a rule, policy, or procedures manual) are preparing the time card at the end of each workday, notifying the personnel office in case of on-the-job sickness, and keeping the work area neat and clean. These things take up worker's time; therefore, they should be in the JD and the employees should be evaluated on how well they do them.

WHY CATEGORIZE DUTIES?

In the preceding discussion of activity categories some good reasons for categorizing as in Figure 1 were hinted at. Now the discussion will be a bit more involved and cite some powerful, general reasons for this formatting or categorizing approach.

Identifies More Fundamental Elements of Structure

Formatting a JD by basic categories of activities is like identifying the basic structural components—the frame—of a building or bridge. You cannot understand what holds the building together by looking only at the walls, ceiling, and floor. You have to look beneath to more basic elements of design. Identifying activity categories helps in analysis of the more fundamental components of the design of a job. Since categorizing lumps tasks similar in certain characteristics together, it speeds and simplifies study of those tasks. It provides you with a higher level of analysis, which contributes to deeper insight into the structure of the job. Categorizing shows the major dimensions of the job and how smaller dimensions relate. A random listing of tasks does not provide this key structural data. Because formatting leads you to better interpretation of the nature of a job, it facilitates improving the design of the job.

Allows for Better Comparison of Jobs and Performance

Establishing categories that can be used to describe any job gives you common dimensions along which to compare the nature of different jobs. You can better compare jobs with respect to work loads and volumes of different classes of task demands. When you can better determine the relative demands imposed by different jobs, you can set more equitable rewards for jobs. By having common dimensions along which to compare jobs you can better assure that jobs that are more difficult, jobs that are more dangerous, jobs that require the exercise of greater authority do, in fact, pay more than jobs that demand less of the worker.

Breaking jobs down into the same major classes of activities not only eases the task of job evaluation—determining the relative worth of jobs for pay and benefits determination purposes—it also helps in comparing the performance of different workers on different jobs because it gives you a set of structural dimensions common to all jobs. Performance differentials become more vivid and thus pay on the basis of performance can be made more equitable.

Helps Assure Key Task Areas Are Drawn Out in Job Analysis

Identifying major classes of activities in the JD and communicating these to employees during job analysis can help draw out from employees all types of activities engaged in by them. Job analyses often rely on self-reporting of activities/responsibilities by employees. Frequently employees have trouble remembering or recognizing all their tasks or all the ways in which they spend their time. Formatting, as described here, can stimulate recall and recognition, helping assure a complete job activity profile is provided by each employee on the job analysis questionnaire or during the job analysis interview. A properly formatted JD can help in subsequent job analysis efforts as much as job analysis helps prepare JDs.

Helps Employees Better Understand Their Jobs

New employees, particularly, are often bewildered by the scores of different tasks for which they find themselves responsible. They can often make little sense out of the apparent random array of tasks. Patterns of tasks and task relationships are often not readily discernible. Distributing tasks in the JD by major categories helps one quickly to grasp the scope of the job and to find meaningfulness in the nature of the job. In short, breaking a job into a few major activity categories helps one make sense out of the job quickly. This means the new recruit can be assimilated into the organization faster.

Identifies Task Areas Requiring Similar Skills

Developing major task categories means lumping tasks that are similar, in some respect, together. Each task in a given activity category usually requires at least some of the same skills or talents as other tasks in that category. By categorizing you can tell how many different tasks require similar abilities and kinds of training. This can help you determine the desirability and content of training. Priority can be given to training programs developed around "full" activity categories. Execution of all tasks in a category can be addressed by a given training program. Without task categorizing, training programs may fail to encompass reference to important tasks that should be included because of the type of skill they require. Task categorizing helps show the different major classes of skills that a job requires. Consequently, it aids in developing more relevant training programs.

Identifies Task Areas
Requiring Different Means for Performance Assessment

Different parts of a given job may require different means for assessing the employee's performance. Too frequently, we try to use one instrument, one evaluator, or one method to evaluate all employee performance along all task dimensions. This typically results in invalid appraisals along some dimensions. With task categorizing, activities with similar characteristics are identified. This helps in adapting assessment methodology to different phases of the job. For example, one's performance in group work can often be best assessed by other group members; one's performance on non-supervisory tasks can usually be assessed properly by one's superior; one's performance on unplanned work may be best assessed by an independent observer or outside consultant. The point is that performance on activities in each different category may require different modes of assessment. Categorization helps pinpoint specific means of assessment that are most appropriate for different kinds of activities.

Forces a Full Disclosure of Time Usage

Activity formatting that recognizes non-work/semi-work activities and unplanned work forces development of a complete and accurate profile of how the human resource is being used. It shows fully how one's time on the job is spent. These categories of time usage are typically ignored in the classical JD. The classical attempt is to account for 100 percent of a worker's time by allocating time only to planned work. This results in false representation of how time is actually spent.

Categorizing activities also makes it easier to determine how much time is allocated to different activities. In a job analysis it is often difficult to determine exactly how much time to allocate to specific tasks, but an estimate of time for an entire class of activities can be relatively easily established. Realistic time estimation for each of twenty-five or thirty tasks is a simpler task if first a time allocation is determined for each of the major categories for which individual tasks are a part.

Formatting provides a depth of analysis, an understanding, and an appreciation missing from the classical JD. The format described in the previous section is not the only possible format, however. Activities may be classed in literally dozens of different, but useful, ways. The format described in this chapter does offer some special utilities that others do not.

HOW TO ORDER AND WRITE DUTY STATEMENTS

How the duty statement section is written is critical for understanding the real meaning of the work. It should be noted before reading further that here the terms *duty* and *task* are used interchangeably. Many writers define duties as larger in scope than tasks. That is, a duty may consist of numerous tasks. This distinction is not made here.

Itemized Duty Statements

Itemized duty, or task, statements are better for describing a job than a narrative description because such statements separate the job into distinctive elements. Each task statement represents a unique, relatively self-contained component of the total job to be done. Numbering each statement in the list is better than lettering because a quick glance tells the reader just how many distinctive components of the job have been identified.

Categorized Duty Statements

It is useful for illustrating the structure of a job to, as suggested earlier, categorize duty statements. Within each category, task (duty) statements should be arranged by priority—the most important task being listed first, the least important last. This helps the employee focus on key areas when reading the JD because one reads from top to bottom.

A Comprehensive Listing

It is possible in writing task statements to lump a number of different duties together into a single statement. This practice, though perhaps helping to simplify and shorten the JD, is not appropriate for clarifying the design of the work. Separate duties should be listed separately and as many different statements incorporated in the JD as is required to describe the whole job. Nothing should be left out.

As discussed earlier, it is often desirable to classify duties into major functional areas of responsibility. This aids immeasurably in interpreting the structure of a job. It is usually wise to attach an "Other" category (or statement), as in Appendix A, at the end of the list of major functions to cover responsibilities not properly covered by previous statements and to allow for duty assignment flexibility—that is, to allow for assignment of additional duties if so required. Note in Appendix A that the "Other" category has been used to cover other routine items, temporary tasks, unplanned tasks, group tasks, and non-work/semi-work.

Accuracy and Detail

In writing individual duty statements care must be taken to achieve accuracy, to choose words that are readable and clearly communicate the meaning of the duty, and to give enough information and sufficient detail to fully describe the duty. There is no definitive rule as to how much detail to build in. Detail sufficient to generate, for the person unacquainted with the duty, true understanding of the duty is what is necessary. Remember, however, that a JD is not a description of methods—not an elaborate write-up on how-to-do. Brevity has its virtues and the preparer of a JD must avoid the overly elaborate statement. Concise and to the point is the order.

Action Verbs and Expected Results

All duty statements should start with an action verb in the present tense such as: plans, assembles, writes, negotiates, tests. Avoid vague, too general verbs such as: engages, handles, acts, does. Action verbs at the beginning quickly inform the reader of the kind of action the person is engaged in. Properly chosen verbs tell, with some precision, what the person does. Each statement should also reflect an objective—what is to be accomplished—what results, outcomes, or outputs are expected—either explicitly stated or implied. Identifiable units of work should appear in these duty statements; unnecessary information should be avoided. Statements should exhibit a terse, direct writing style.

Description of the Depth and Scope of Duties

In writing duty statements attention should be given to incorporating critical data that define the depth and scope of the duty. Some of the kinds of data that are often useful to include are: (1) data on resources—tools, equipment, materials, facilities, and information the person uses to execute the duty; (2) data on where the duty takes place; (3) data on who else might be involved in the duty (who shares in execution, who receives output, etc.); (4) data on when or with what frequency the duty is executed; (5) data on duty regularity; and (6) data on the conditions under which the duty is performed. Duty statements must help describe the volume of work—a type of condition—as well as the environmental conditions such as the physical, social, political, technical, and economic climates under which the work is performed. Just describing *what* is done does not depict the full design of the work.

Sample Duty Statements

Following are some sample duty statements for a typical supervisor who also performs some operative work:

1. Schedules work for one week using the Tandy 1000 in his or her secretary's office each Monday for each of five subordinates, and communicates each worker's assignment to him or her by written interoffice memo prior to 10:00 A.M. on Mondays.
2. Counsels employees in his or her department to resolve work-related problems that are brought to attention by the employees themselves. Such problems develop at random and average about five per week.
3. Conducts evaluations in mid-January and mid-July using a company-authorized instrument prepared by the Personnel Department, to identify developmental needs of each employee in the department.
4. Starts up machine number 2 in plant section B, to assure operation of the entire line, on the first and third Saturdays of each month.
5. Files official institutional documents on policy development received from the Personnel Office, in file number 3 in his or her secretary's office.
6. Picks up and delivers crates by fork-lift from incoming trucks parked at the loading dock to the cold storage facility. Does not stack the crates inside the facility.
7. Decides subordinate requests for time off when time requested is not part of the annual vacation.
8. Prepares, with input from all subordinates, the annual department budget on prepared forms submitted by the Accounting Office.

Notice the use of the word *to* in duty statements numbers 2, 3, and 4 above. This word allows you to specifically identify a result or desired objective within the duty statement. One engages in the action specified by the beginning action verb to achieve the result stated later on in the statement.

Note that in item 2 a second sentence is provided to add important data about the timing and volume of work of this type. Note in item 6 that a second sentence is provided for clarity purposes to assure the worker knows the boundaries or limits of his or her job. Task items may include more than one sentence if such adds to the clarity or completeness of the description. Note also that some of the statements indicate where the work is done, some indicate when the work is done, and some indicate task or equipment used.

Suppose an employee has the task of troubleshooting. In the JD you could write: "Troubleshoots problems." This really says very little. You should indicate what kind of problems, where in the organization, how frequently, and so on. A better approach would be to present the following statement series: "Troubleshoots electrical system problems, in manufacturing room number 1, to get systems quickly back on line. Initiates troubleshooting at request of machine workers and employs foreman A as an aid. Such problems require about two hours time on the average and occur at the rate of approximately ten per month."

TIME AND PRIORITY DISTRIBUTIONS

Time and priority distributions are two kinds of absolutely essential data, more often than not left out of real-world JDs.

Use Time Percentages

In a recent study done by the writer, 90 percent of the job descriptions surveyed listed tasks but gave no information on either how long it took to do

Figure 2
Matrix Formatted JD

Task No.	Nature of Task	% of Time	Importance (1-10)	Frequency	Average Time Per Cycle	Others Involved
1	Delivers boxes	25%	3	2 times/ day	1 hr.	1 helper
2	Prepares reports	15%	6	1/month	26 hrs.	none
3	Motivates workers	38%	9	12 times/ day	.25 hrs.	27 work- ers

each of the tasks or on the relative importance of each of the tasks. Simple listings of tasks without acknowledging the approximate time consumption per task can be very misleading. They do not truly depict the nature of the work. In one job description surveyed, twenty-two tasks were listed. During an interview with the worker on this job it was discovered that over 80 percent of his time was spent on the third task in the list. Certainly the list alone did not tell the true story. By adding time percentages you can tell what demands on the job are really like.

Consider what attaching a time percentage to the task category "Executes other tasks as required by the supervisor" can do for your understanding of the job. It can really show just how structured and definitive the content of a job is. For example, 60 percent attached to this category would tell you the job is relatively undefined. Appendix A shows a JD with time percentages attached.

Indicate Task Importance

It is also valuable to indicate (say on a scale of one to ten) just how important each task in the worker's task repertoire is. With a small effort the supervisor, together with the workers and perhaps other higher level managers, can decide

Figure 2 (*continued*)

Complexity (1-10)	Error Proba- bility	Tools Used	Outcomes Expected	Where Performed	Hazards	Degree of Decision Making
2	.05	Fork- lift	Safely stacked in inventory	Factory warehouse	Fumes	Low
6	.20	Type- writer	Profes- sional documents for stock- holders	Office	None	High
7	.40	None	High effort exerted	Factory warehouse	None	Medium

task priorities. Not always are those tasks that consume the most time the most important. Often a decision-making task, which takes only a small percentage of an employee's time, will be judged much more important than some operative task that occupies a high percentage of time. It is important to acknowledge the relative importance of tasks to guide the employees when, for example, they are pressured or bottled up with work and must allow some things to slip. Attached priorities help tell the workers what must be attended to and what can be avoided (at least in the short run). Appendix A shows a JD with task importance indexes attached.

MATRIX FORMAT

Matrix formatted JDs are used in some companies. They have some advantages over the more conventional JD described above but, as yet, are not nearly as popular. The primary advantages of a matrix format are that data are systematically displayed and each task is given standardized treatment. All tasks are described with the same kinds of data. When this is done it is relatively simple to compare tasks and different jobs. Comparison of tasks within a job may be important in establishing task priorities and when considering job redesign among other things. Comparison of jobs is essential, for example, in establishing equitable pay. Figure 2 is a sample matrix format for a JD.

This type of JD does not involve preparation of written statements. It assures, however, that a considerable amount of relevant data for each task will be presented without resort to full statements. The tabular presentation allows for rapid identification and comparison of a number of pertinent dimensions of individual task designs. Such a description can be developed for any kind of managerial job as well as for any type of operative job. It may take a little longer to prepare this kind of instrument, however.

The matrix format can easily be expanded to show other bits of information relevant to tasks that are not properly conceptualized as part of the job design but are nonetheless useful data items. For example, person specs and performance criteria can easily be indicated for each task by adding just two more columns. Minimum, or desired, levels (standards) for person specs and performance criteria can also be added. Many firms recognize the value of having all this vital data in one document. The wealth of job-related data and the orderly display of that data made possible by a matrix format can immensely improve the utility of the job description for managing the human resource. Analysis and quantification of job-related information are greatly facilitated with this type of display.

CHAPTER 4

How to Gather Data for Preparation of the Job Description

The rigorous methodology of science must be pursued when gathering data for any purpose, if those data are to be regarded as complete and valid. Organizations generally invest heavily in funding data gathering in basic and applied research activities that have a visible, physical product payoff. Likewise, dollar and cents data gathering is generally sufficiently funded for purposes of preparing accurate accounting records and financial statements. Data gathering for human resource management, however, is often not highly funded in organizations, though there is some evidence of a change in attitude on this matter.

At present few organizations really worry much about gathering comprehensive and accurate job data. There is much evidence of this across organizations of all types and sizes. Job data-gathering efforts tend to be buried within obscure sections of personnel departments and data-gathering methodologies tend to be replete with departures from the scientific method.

Some of the reason for the relative lack of attention to rigor in job data gathering can be traced to the desire of managers to leave the boundaries of jobs in their authority domains underdefined for the purpose of enhancing their own social power within the organization. Lack of job definition means to many managers that they are relatively free to bend and shape to suit their personal interests and objectives; but what may be best for the individual manager may not be best for the organization as a whole. Organizations should attend much more thoroughly to job data gathering. This chapter points out what should be done.

GENERAL PRINCIPLES OF DATA GATHERING

Too often the job analysis—the term given to the process of gathering data about jobs—is conducted by the novice. Someone assumes this kind of work requires relatively little experience. Little could be further from the truth. The job description is only as good—only as useful—as the quality of the data collected to write it, and contemporary data-collection methodology is fraught with opportunity for serious errors. To properly avoid these errors requires considerable experience and skill. A number of data-gathering principles must be carefully adhered to.

Gather Data from Multiple Sources

Too frequently job data gathering focuses exclusively on acquiring information about the job from the job incumbent. True, no other single person is likely to know as much about the job as does the incumbent; but the incumbent is not the only one likely to possess valuable insights into the job. Fellow workers— peers, supervisors, subordinates, and people in other departments with whom the worker interacts—can provide unique insights and different perspectives on what a given worker does. The information gathered from these other sources is not as likely to be biased or distorted toward the self-interest of incumbents.

Certainly a key person in job data acquisition is the supervisor. Supervisors should always be consulted when compiling data about jobs in their departments, because they generally know better than anyone what the work *should* be like. They can often help clarify task boundaries—where one person's job leaves off and another starts. Supervisors can usually add much to preparing job function statements, to specifying the limits of workers' independent authority, and to establishing key accountabilities. Supervisors should fill out job analysis questionnaires on their subordinates and should be interviewed about the jobs of each of their subordinates. They may not be able to contribute significantly to the development of detailed duty statements unless they have actually performed the work, at some point in time, themselves.

Another good source of data about jobs is persons who have recently left their jobs. These people have little to accomplish by coloring the nature of the work. They serve as a second source of direct data about the job that can be used to verify data from the present jobholder.

Information from people other than the incumbent may help catch some aspects of work missed by the incumbent and will serve to verify data received from the incumbent. When data from different sources do not seem to be compatible, the analyst can investigate to find the cause of the discrepancy and then take action to assure data consistency.

Gather Data by Multiple Means

Often job analyses will focus exclusively on gathering data by one means only. The questionnaire distributed to job incumbents is common. This method, though as effective singularly as any, will not assure complete and valid data when used alone. The analyst should always follow up the filled in questionnaire with an interview to clarify data provided by the incumbent and to check on the quality of data submitted.

Other means of data acquisition such as work logs and work sampling usually yield valuable data totally ignored by the incumbent when filling out a questionnaire. These devices are particularly good at gaining insight into the frequency of task execution, time spent on tasks, and the sequences of task execution. Questionnaires and interviews do not provide high-quality information on these matters.

If a complete, detailed picture of work is needed, filming or direct, continuous observation may be the only way to acquire complete, valid data. These methods can be disruptive and distort true behavior but usually if the observed worker is properly prepared, filming or direct observation will yield valid data.

It is too common for *no* means at all to be used for data gathering. That is, the incumbent, or the incumbent's supervisor, is asked to sit down and directly prepare, from memory, a job description for the incumbent. Preparing a JD in this manner usually does not work well because the preparer is not likely to be able to think of all that should go into the JD without some kind of search for data coupled with extensive deliberation. Formal data gathering preliminary to JD preparation helps assure key parts of the work are not left out.

Do Time-extended Data Gathering

No job data-gathering activity ever succeeded when it was rushed. Workers, supervisors of workers, and others need time to think through jobs in order to fill out questionnaires properly and to participate effectively in interviews. In fact many jobs change by month or by season. Therefore having employees fill out questionnaires and participate in interviews over just a one- or two-week period may not elicit from respondents a true picture of year-round activity.

Similarly, filming, direct observation, work samples, and work logs conducted over too short a time span will not provide a picture of fluctuations in job content and context over time. You need an adequate sample of behavior taken over a period of time that covers, at a minimum, one complete work cycle. If multiple cycles can be studied, the quality of the data is further improved.

No job analysis should force the employee to provide data too quickly. Workers should not have to cram data providing in and around other tasks or feel excessive pressure to submit data by a specific date. Data gathering should not take time away from other important tasks the worker must do. When this happens, the worker is hurried to submit data and consequently submits data laden with error. If the job analysis is so important—and it is—it should be given the time it deserves. Indeed, providing data for the job analysis should be a duty built into the worker's job design. A certain amount of time—company time—should be allotted for it. It is not wise to request employees to generate job data on their personal, away-from-work time.

Prepare Data Providers

Those who provide data about a job do not provide comprehensive and accurate data when they are not trained properly. Data providers should be fully instructed, prior to execution of data-gathering procedures, about how to fill out any instruments that will be used such as questionnaires and work logs, how to word task statements submitted on questionnaires, what to include in task statements, at what intervals they should stop work and record job analysis data, and so on. They need to be thoroughly oriented on the various means by which data will be gathered, the various sources from which data will be acquired, and on the rationale for consulting different sources and using different means. This enhances their receptivity to the process.

Data givers should understand that job analysis takes time and that it will prove frustrating from time to time. Analysts may repeat questions and probe for clarity to a point that irritates respondents. Supervisors and subordinates may well not agree on what a job is like. Time will have to be taken to resolve these differences.

Those providing data about a job need to be motivated to do so, too. They need to be told why the data are being collected—to what uses the data will be put. Someone, preferably top management, must convince them that all levels of management support the job analysis effort and that such an effort will bring substantial benefits to the employee and to the company. These benefits should be thoroughly discussed with employees.

A plan for granting employees rewards contingent on the quality of their efforts during job analysis should be developed and communicated to the employees. Also, employees should be informed on what problems to expect during the process and on help that is available to them during the process. Further, management would do well to assure employees they will receive full feedback on the results of the data-gathering effort and on any documents, such as job descriptions, generated from the data.

Intervene in the Process

Above all, managers and/or analysts must not assume a job data-gathering effort will run by itself. Intervention is necessary to control the process—to keep it on schedule and to assure quality data come in. Providers of data *will* need help. They will have questions that need answering.

Unless the analyst, or management, establishes clear checkpoints for certain data to be turned in, the process can easily slip behind. What often happens, for example, is that employees will save up their recording of data on instruments until the end of the day or week. Letting time slip by like this means that when the data are recorded they are not as fresh in the minds of workers and, therefore, not as accurate. Such data as from work logs and work samples should be collected daily to spot any problems and to assure they are being recorded regularly.

Intervention is also useful to keep worker motivation established prior to the actual data gathering from slipping. During data acquisition, workers can be praised for their efforts, given special opportunities to sit down and fill out data forms, given privileges for on-time submittal of data.

The point is, be sure not to assume that the data-gathering operation will run by itself. It will not. It needs regular attention. It needs intrusive management that actively intervenes to dig out problems rather than passive management standing by and waiting to be told about problems. Problems often do not come to light without investigation and prodding.

Use Participation in Planning

When employees participate in formulating basic parameters of the job analysis effort, they understand the effort better and are more willing to accept it. After all, participative planning means the plan is part theirs. Instrumentation and specific techniques for data acquisition should be *decided* by the analyst but employees can provide useful insight into what kinds of instruments and techniques might best be used. Sometimes work logs, for example, are just not appropriate. It may not be practical for the worker to stop periodically and to record activity up to that point. Sometimes filming may be the *only* good way to get data. When, for example, precise time percentages must be attached to tasks, filming is probably essential. Workers, themselves, can provide valuable insight here.

Almost always workers can provide useful information on questionnaire construction. They can help word questions such that they will be clearly understood. Almost always the workers should decide *when* to conduct the analysis—what times are convenient for them. In scheduling data gathering by log, questionnaire, or interview, for example, the analyst must recognize the other time demands on the worker. The worker should have considerable voice in the process.

Workers can further participate in the job analysis planning effort by suggesting problems that they or others may encounter—problems of stress, of motivation, of lack of time, related to lack of data reliability and validity, and so on. After all, the workers know their jobs better and know better how the job analysis will fit their work situations than does the analyst. The analyst needs their guidance.

Focus on Usage of Time

Data gathering must not focus only on what formal, official tasks the worker engages in. Much work is unplanned and much of a worker's day is spent doing things other than formally delegated tasks. In job analysis we want to uncover truth in design. We are interested in idle time, fatigue time, planned and unintentional delays, interstation travel time, non-work (on-the-job) engagements, and more. A complete picture of work comes only from an analysis of how *time* is used. Therefore, the worker must be encouraged when filling out work logs and questionnaires to incorporate non-productive time and semi-productive time as well as productive time. How total time in the day is used will tell us what the job's design is really like. For example, one may have fifty different tasks that are performed daily but one-half of the day may be spent idle. Just noting the duties does not tell us what this job is like.

Workers must be encouraged to focus on how they use their time rather than on just what duties or responsibilities they have if we are to get a clear picture of opportunities or needs for job redesign. Obviously a job with excessive delay time would be a candidate for adding tasks. A job with no idle time, or fatigue time, might well be a candidate for deleting tasks. Jobs that require extensive worker in-plant travel might well be candidates for redesign. Perhaps tasks could be located physically closer together. Jobs that involve excessive daily social interaction might well be changed by altering the social environments of those jobs. Focusing on duties instead of time usage tends to encourage workers to fill up their days, on paper, with duties to which 100 percent of the workday time is allotted. Anyone knows that it is rare to have 100 percent of one's workday filled with official duties.

Work Down from the Supervisor

Where do you start in job analysis interviews? If a number of jobs are to be analyzed, a good practice is to start at the administrative top of the heap and work down. In interviewing job incumbents, interviewing the top manager in a group first gives you broad insight into the jobs underneath. You gain significant knowledge of *all* jobs in his or her department. This gives you greater savvy as you move throughout the department gathering data by interview.

You can ask supervisors in one interview not only about their jobs but also about the jobs of their subordinates. They will likely give you many points to pursue in subsequent interviewing of those subordinates. Interview the supervisor first, but when you conduct this interview be sure all other means of data collection have already been pursued. You should have work log data, questionnaire data, and so on for all people in the department, including the supervisor, prior to the interview. The interview is to provide opportunity to probe certain areas in depth—to clarify nebulous areas.

After the manager of a department is interviewed, interview his or her subordinates and then, in turn, the subordinates of those subordinates. This gives you a systematic top-to-bottom process that provides maximum preparation for the analyst prior to any given interview.

Use Standardized Procedures

To assure objective accumulation of data, to help assure fair treatment of all employees participating in a job analysis, and to promote ease of comparison of data acquired on different jobs, the same instruments and procedures for gathering data should be used, whenever possible, across all employees covered by the study. Sometimes variations will be necessary if one job differs in structure substantially from another. For example, it may make good sense to film a machine operator, but a questionnaire may be best for the all-purpose laborer. A strong attempt should be made to acquire the same kind of data for each job. At a minimum, a job data-collection program must be coordinated by one person or a central office to assure equal and fair treatment of subjects in the process.

Have Repeated and Ongoing Acquisition of Data

JDs must never be looked upon as cast in cement. They can always be refined and improved. Furthermore, jobs do not stay static. JD change should be the norm. This means that data gathering must never stop. It must be a regular, ongoing effort. You do not need to run in-depth, formal job analyses every other week but you do need to create systems whereby information on job changes, and information that better describes the job, can be easily generated and regularly funneled to someone responsible for keeping JDs current. Every other year or so it may be wise to conduct—from scratch—a full, formal job analysis.

Have Adaptability of Approach

The best way to gather job data is something that depends highly on the nature of the work and the nature of the workers being studied. It also depends heavily on time availability and cost considerations. Even though standardization of procedure is important, different groups of employees within the same organization may have to be confronted with different data-gathering methods. Or a given group of workers may have to be studied with one method at one point in time and another method at another point in time because of changing circumstances. No one approach is always best. The analyst will have to be flexible and adjust to the situation. This could even mean going so far as to pursue a particular approach to data gathering because it is what the incumbents want.

Use Structured Data Solicitation

No job analysis effort will succeed if it is not carefully planned well in advance. Determination of exactly what information must be acquired, by what means, and when are critical components of the data acquisition plan. Structured questionnaires, interviews, and work logs—if planned and executed properly—can truly stimulate workers' thinking about the job and serve to draw out points that might otherwise remain forever hidden. Asking the right questions in the right way is pivotally significant. Also using a planned, structured approach helps assure the necessary standardization of treatment of various employees mentioned above.

PROCEDURE FOR GATHERING AND ASSEMBLING THE DATA

This section will identify a systematic process for acquiring job data and preparing the JD. To make job analyses successful takes planning and requires some structure. Employees soon think the job analysis is a waste of time if they perceive a disorderly, disjointed effort at gathering the data.

Establish Need for Job Analysis

Your job analysis is doomed to failure if you do not first determine a clear need for it. You must identify the reasons you need such data. For what purposes do you intend to use the data? Not doing this first means you are whistling in the wind. Employees whose jobs are being analyzed will not take you seriously unless you communicate to them why the job analysis is being conducted. Top management cannot possibly support a job analysis effort without clear rationale. Are you gathering job data to help in writing job descriptions, to help in preparing person specifications, or what? If you are acquiring data for job descriptions, what do you want for JD structure and content? What will the JD be used for? All this should be clear to top management, analysts, and employees involved in the analysis.

Perhaps the job data are needed to accurately fill out wage surveys or to submit to outside investigating agencies. Perhaps usage of the data will be to gain insights into how to measure performance so that a contingent reward system can be established. Whatever the uses of the job data, they should be articulated, documented, and communicated. The purposes of a job analysis will help determine how to conduct the study and just what data need to be collected.

Decide Which Jobs to Cover

Next the boundaries of the data-gathering effort have to be decided. Usually not all jobs in the organization have to be covered—only those jobs for which job data are needed. It may be that the organization has reason to cover those operative and managerial jobs within just one department or division, or it may be the organization wishes to analyze all jobs at one given level in the organization—vaulting across departmental boundaries but covering only a certain operative or managerial level.

The rationale for doing a job analysis should give clues as to what positions should be studied. The geographical dispersion of jobs will be another factor in determining what jobs to scrutinize in a given study. How much the company can invest in such a study is a third factor affecting just which kinds of jobs and how many jobs should be covered. One other factor that will help in determining the boundaries of your study is the quality of present job descriptions. If JDs in certain areas have been kept up-to-date regularly, there is little need for additional extensive data gathering in those areas.

Get Management Support

Once the manager, or analyst doing the study, has isolated positions for investigation, he or she must sell the need for the study to top management and those managers on down the line who will be affected by the study. Often high-level management people will be involved in development of the rationale for the study and identification of the positions to be studied. When this is the case, management is likely to need little additional convincing that the study must go forward. Equally often, however, management will not sense the need for a study. Therefore, the analyst must persuade management. Not only must the analyst convince management of the desirability of a job analysis, but the analyst must also get top management to come forth and publicly state its belief in the merits of the project. Management should present a strong case for the value of the study to all those affected by the study. Management should communicate to employees that the project has high priority and that the employees will be given the time they need to fully participate. Management should also point out how the organization intends to use the data acquired and how this data will benefit both the company and the employees. When employees know that management is involved, and is supportive of the analysis effort, they will take it seriously. When employees think such a project is the harebrained scheme of some staff person or some not-so-prominent an individual within the organization, they are likely to balk. Getting top management's support and making sure that support is communicated to all subjects in the study is critical.

Develop Your Methods and Sources

Once you have full support for the project from management, it makes sense to invest time and energy in developing the methods and sources you will use to acquire data. It may take considerable time and money to develop questionnaires, arrange for filming or direct observation, or to develop structured interviews, for example.

What methods and sources you will use depend on the kind of information you want, the types of jobs being studied, the number of jobs being studied, how much help the analyst has, the time frame within which the study must take place, the discipline level of the employees to be studied, and the like. You will want to use multiple methods to assure data validity. It is essential that you acquire input from those affected by the study as to which methods seem to make the most sense for their particular situations. The management of departments covered by the analysis may have preference for one data-gathering device over another and such preferences should be considered and incorporated if at all practical.

A critical point in selecting data-gathering methods and in designing instruments to gather data is to first define precisely what kind and amount of data you want. Deciding the desired structure and content of your JD will suggest how to go about gathering data for its preparation. What information do you wish to present in the JD? At a minimum you will want to gather data on what the worker does, when, where, with whom, with what resources, and for what purpose. Though JDs do not tell *how* work is done, a good job analysis may ask questions about how because knowledge of how often helps clarify *what* is done. You must also decide from just whom—subordinates, peers, supervisors—you want to gather data about a job. Multiple sources assure higher validit;.

Orient the Employees

This is the critical fifth step in the procedure. It was mentioned earlier as a principle of data gathering, so relatively little will be said here about orienting. You engage in orienting the employees only after data-gathering devices and systems have been fairly well resolved. It is probably best to hold a meeting to inform all participants in the project of what is going to take place and why. The meeting can be used to answer questions about the analysis and to allay fears some incumbents may have. Employees sometimes fear job analysis because they think it will result in putting them in a straightjacket or they think management must believe they are doing something wrong to invest so much in such a study.

The key point for orientation is to remember that all participants need to be trained and motivated to perform well as subjects in the study. This means considerable discussion of how to use instruments like logs and questionnaires, as well as considerable discussion of the many valuable ways in which gathered data will be used by the organization. Make sure supervisors involved in the analysis know that the analysis is going to take a substantial amount of their time. They will be called on for data for their own jobs plus data for all jobs in their departments.

Schedule and Sequence Data Gathering

Input from subjects on when to schedule data acquisition by work logs, interviews, filmings, and such must be encouraged. Data gathering that interferes with other work assignments will result in those other assignments being neglected as well as in faulty data for the study. Employees can tell you when they can best fit in their data-providing obligations.

Once employee input has been received—and this can start during the previous orientation period—a firm, time-lined schedule should be developed. When the study will begin and end, when subjects are supposed to turn in logs and questionnaires, when observations and filmings will take place, or whatever, should be formulated and clearly communicated to subjects in advance. This will allow employees time to rearrange some of their activities to accommodate the time constraints of the study. Of course the analyst must remain flexible. Not always, for example, will you be able to conduct interviews as scheduled. However, need to deviate from your schedule should be rare if proper planning is done.

In addition to proper timing, it is important to sequence the multiple methods you use to gather data. Time logs are good to run ahead of questionnaires because they help get workers to see what they are doing before they have to answer questions about this in the questionnaire. Questionnaires ought to be completed before interviews are conducted. There are some methods such as work sampling and filming that can be implemented at most any time and yield full, rich data.

Sequencing sources, as well as methods, may be important too. Information gathered from certain sources can lead you to fuller data generation from other sources. For example, it is generally best to interview incumbents about their jobs before interviewing the peers of incumbents.

Formulating and sticking to a schedule and a predetermined sequence in data gathering will help assure that all subjects are treated the same during the analysis. It will help assure that the analysis is, in fact, completed and that it does not "drift" into other time frames, causing unexpected interference with operations as well as the generation of suspect data.

Gather the Data

After time lines have been set, the actual gathering of data can begin. The analyst, manager, or other persons charged with assuring time lines are adhered to must monitor the data-gathering process to make sure questionnaires, logs, and other forms come in according to plan. If some incumbents fail to submit certain data, they must be reminded promptly and urged to get the material in as soon as is possible.

Analysts, or others, must remain available to provide help to subjects who may have problems or difficulties developing the written data required for questionnaires, logs, and forms. As mentioned earlier, ideally the analyst would initiate contact with subjects to spot any developing difficulties before serious problems arise.

The analyst, or others guiding the project, must be sensitive to incumbent attitudes and motivation during the data acquisition process and initiate any action required to keep up subject desire to see the process through. For example, sometimes an analyst can arrange for another employee to take over one's job while that person is being interviewed. This may create a positive attitude on the part of the subject because he or she will be assured that while they are being interviewed a burdensome work backlog is not piling up. Above all, the point is that the process of gathering data must be controlled.

Resolve Discrepancies in Data

Once all data are collected from all sources and by all planned means, they must be scrutinized for inconsistencies and possible errors. If, for example, data collected about the incumbent's job by interview with the incumbent do not agree with data collected about the incumbent's job by interview with the incumbent's supervisor, then discussions—perhaps a meeting with analyst, supervisor, and incumbent present—must be held to resolve the differences. Similarly, if data collected by work log from the incumbent do not agree with data collected by interview with the incumbent, action must be pursued to resolve differences.

The resolution of discrepancies can take considerable man-hours and may be an extremely frustrating and somewhat embarrassing process for those involved. But this effort is at the heart of developing accurate pictures of the work. It is because data by different means and from different sources are not likely to be the same that job analysis should involve multiple means and sources. One source and means serves as a check on another.

If discrepancies are too serious, it may be necessary to redo the study of the job or to pursue data with other data-gathering devices and from other sources. Sometimes intensive interviewing can resolve such discrepancies. Sometimes bringing other parties, familiar with the job or peripherally associated with the job, into an in-depth discussion can resolve the problem. Usually substantial additional analysis will be required.

Write a Preliminary Job Description

After the data are accumulated by all means from all sources, and discrepancies resolved, the analyst can put together a coherent description of the design of the job. This description should be an accurate reflection of how the incumbent actually uses his or her time. It should show the actual work environment, actual tools and equipment, actual accountabilities, actual independent authority exercised, and so on. This description should not represent an attempt to shape the job into a desired design or to distort the real picture of work to show what the ideal would be like. Though this is a preliminary JD, it should contain all the sections, all the types of information, and well-written task statements just as if it were a final description.

This document must be a complete and accurate description of what *is*. It should be circulated between superior and subordinate with adjustments in content and structure continually made until both agree that it is a full and accurate representation of the job's design. The analyst will often want to help this refinement effort by doing additional interviewing or other data gathering to clarify unclear points.

In writing JDs it can be extremely helpful to do a number of related JDs at once. The insights gained in writing one JD will lead to better understanding of what should be written in the other JDs. Understanding of a given job can be highly enhanced by building one's understanding of related or associated jobs—that is, jobs in the same department or at the same organizational level.

Write a Final Prescription

Once the preliminary JD has been finished, the supervisor with input from higher levels, the subordinate, and others in the department must carefully study the present design to see if it is the one that should exist. The design pictured in the preliminary JD is the actual design. This must be compared with what the organization thinks the design should be like.

Study of the actual design may reveal numerous opportunities for improvement. Perhaps tasks should be added or subtracted from the job. Perhaps it becomes apparent that too much time is being spent in certain areas. Perhaps investigation will reveal that the frequency of contacts with others is excessive or that the independent authority of the position is inadequate. At any rate, it is very likely that opportunities for improvement will be found.

Any desired changes in job design should be made and written into a final job prescription identifying what should occur on the job—not what can occur, not what will occur, and not what does occur. These changes must be communicated to the incumbent and his or her acceptance of the changes must be acquired.

Date and Get Signatures

Once the final job prescription is established and agreed to by all relevant parties, the prescription should be dated and signed by the incumbent, the supervisor, and any other approving authorities such as the head of personnel or some higher echelon manager. It may also be wise to have the analyst or preparer of the final JD sign it. Too often companies pull out of the file JDs that provide no information on when they were prepared, who prepared them, or who approved them. It is next to impossible to have any faith in the validity of such documents.

Decide Distribution, Storage, Access, Updating Routines, and Use

This is not really part of gathering and assembling the data but is too important a point to neglect to mention. The point is that determination of who gets copies of the JDs, where they will be stored, who will have access to them, how and when they will be used, who will update them and when is vital. Without this the JD development effort is largely a waste.

COMMON METHODS AND SOURCES
FOR DATA GATHERING

Earlier discussions alluded to a variety of data-gathering methods but here each will be elaborated on and illustrated. Some advantages and disadvantages of each will be discussed and some quality methods not hinted at previously will be mentioned. The important point for you to keep in mind is that no one method will do the job for you. It takes a variety of approaches properly planned and scheduled.

Questionnaires

See Appendix H for a sample job analysis questionnaire. Such a questionnaire can be distributed to the worker *and* to the supervisor of the worker. Both subordinate and supervisor can fill in this type of instrument describing the work of the subordinate. The views of both supervisor and subordinate can then be compared, and a more accurate picture of the job developed.

The structure and wording of the questionnaire is critical to stimulate thinking about the job—to stimulate full and accurate responses. For example, questions must be clear, must not confusingly overlap, and must be arranged from the simple to the more complex to ease the burden of responding. No questionnaire should ever be distributed to employees without full orientation provided on the purpose of the questionnaire and how to go about filling it in.

Questionnaires are one of the least costly methods for collecting information. They represent an efficient way to collect a large amount of information in a short period of time. The sample in Appendix H asks questions about the tasks, expected outcomes, abilities and skills required, working conditions, and so forth. A less-structured approach can be used where you ask workers to describe their jobs in their own terms. Each approach has its advantages and disadvantages, but the structured is generally better because it allows for better comparing of data and jobs.

Here are a few additional hints on what to think about when preparing and using questionnaires:

1. *Review questionnaires* used by organizations, professional groups, or university researchers. By reviewing other questionnaires, often you can put together your own in a relatively short period of time. Many items on other questionnaires may not

occur to you before the process begins; thus you can learn from other analysts' experiences.

2. *Keep it short.* Most individuals do not like completing questionnaires. The longer the questionnaire, the less attention will be paid to the items during its completion.

3. *Have each questionnaire completed at work..* Questionnaires that must be completed at home often are not given that earnest effort. As important to the organization as job analysis is, it should be done on company time so that employees have adequate time to provide the information and do not look upon this as an extra burden they must bear.

4. *Categorize answers.* Structure questions so that the responses can be categorized as much as possible. When possible, design closed-end questions; have employees check one of several responses or indicate numbers or percentages for responses whenever possible. This avoids gathering information that is hard to compare or cannot be used by the analyst.

5. *Test the questionnaire* with several trusted employees. Many times the analyst will find that questions may be vague and misleading, or that important aspects of the jobs have been omitted.

6. *Include one open-ended question.* Always include at least one question that allows the employee to give any additional information that has not been transmitted in the rest of the written questionnaire. This may facilitate communication about particular qualities of some jobs.[1]

Interviews

Interviewing the incumbent and the incumbent's supervisor can provide valuable data not derivable by other means. Interviews allow the analyst to motivate accurate responses by fully discussing with the interviewee the rationale for the job analysis effort and the importance of the data collected. They also permit analysts to explain questions and to probe unclear points to a greater depth than would be possible with the questionnaire.

Using group interviews with several employees doing the same kind of work or with the incumbent and employees who regularly interact with him or her (including, perhaps, the supervisor) can be a valuable approach for stimulating honesty in responses and full portrayal of the job. Group interviews can also be used with managers and others to gain insight into given jobs. During group interviews, interviewees will stimulate the thinking of one another about the job. A comment by one person will trigger another comment from someone else. This leads to fuller and more accurate disclosure.

Interviews are most valuable when used in conjunction with other techniques such as questionnaires and work logs so data can be verified. The most worthwhile interview is a structured one with predetermined questions carefully planned and sequenced. This gives the interview direction and helps assure that the same kinds of data are gathered from each different employee interviewed.

If job descriptions are to be standardized across departments, then interview format and content also should be standardized.

Interviews also work best if they are conducted after the analyst has gained insight into a given job by work logs or questionnaires and after the analyst has consulted with the supervisor of the incumbent about the given job. Job analysts are much better prepared to ask worthwhile questions during the interview if they have considerable insight into the job first.

Interviews are expensive; they take time. They also require considerable patience and skill on the part of the analyst. The analyst has to know how to direct the interviewee toward expression of information that will be worthwhile. A useful technique to use during interviews is to ask interviewees to categorize their jobs into six to twelve general areas of responsibility such that all specific tasks will be covered by the general categories—this is a technique that helps employees better visualize and understand their jobs. This gets interviewees to mentally probe the structure of their jobs, and to comprehend the entire job. Such leads to richer discussion later in the interview.

Standardized Questionnaires, Checklists, and Functional Job Analysis

Appendixes I and J illustrate two standardized job analysis questionnaires. Appendix K shows a sample, tailor-made, quantitative task inventory for job analysis.[2] Standardized questionnaires have the advantages of being already developed, fully tested for validity, and allowing for comparison of data across organizations. The fact that jobs in many different types of organizations have essentially the same structure is the underlying rationale for use of standardized approaches. Quantitative task inventories have the great advantage of allowing for in-depth statistical analysis of jobs and for better comparison of jobs.

The Managerial Position Description Questionnaire (MPDQ) is a method of analysis that relies upon the checklist to analyze jobs. It contains 208 items related to the concerns and responsibilities of managers, their demands and restrictions, and miscellaneous characteristics. These 208 items have been condensed into thirteen job factors:

1. Product, market, and financial planning
2. Coordination of other organization units and personnel
3. Internal business control
4. Products and services responsibility
5. Public and customer relations
6. Advanced consulting
7. Autonomy of action
8. Approval of financial commitments
9. Staff service

10. Supervision

11. Complexity and stress

12. Advanced financial responsibility

13. Broad personnel responsibility

The MPDQ is designed for managerial positions, but responses to the items vary by managerial level in any organization and also in different organizations. The MPDQ is appropriate for determining the training needs of employees moving into managerial jobs, evaluating managerial jobs, creating job families and placing new managerial jobs into the right job family, and compensating managerial jobs.

The Position Analysis Questionnaire (PAQ) describes jobs in terms of worker activities. The six activities analyzed in the PAQ are:

1. Information input: Where and how does the worker get the information used in performing the job? Examples are the use of written materials and near-visual differentiation.

2. Mental processes: What reasoning, decision-making, planning, and information-processing activities are involved in performing the job? Examples are the level of reasoning in problem solving and coding/decoding.

3. Work output: What physical activities does the worker perform, and what tools or devices are used? Examples are the use of keyboard devices and assembling/disassembling.

4. Relationships with other people: What relationships with other people are required in performing the job? Examples are instructing and contacts with the public or customers.

5. Job context: In what physical or social contexts is the work performed? Examples are high temperature and interpersonal conflict situations.

6. Other job characteristics: What other activities, conditions, or characteristics are relevant to the job?

The PAQ rates each job on the basis of 194 descriptions related to these six activities. In the PAQ the nature of jobs is essentially determined in terms of communication/decision making/social responsibilities; performance of skilled activities; physical activity and related environmental conditions; operation of vehicles and equipment; and processing of information. Using these five dimensions, jobs can be compared and clustered. The job clusters can then be used for, among other things, staffing decisions and the development of job descriptions and specifications. The PAQ's reliance on person-oriented traits allows it to be applied across a variety of jobs and organizations without modification. This, of course, allows organizations to more easily compare their job analyses with those of other organizations.

The Hay Plan is used in a large number of organizations. Although much less structured than the MPDQ and PAQ, it is systematically tied into a job evaluation and compensation system. Thus use of the Hay Plan allows an organization to maintain consistency not only in how it describes managerial jobs but also in how it rewards them. The purpose of the Hay Plan are management development, placement, recruitment, job evaluation, measurement of the execution of a job against specific standards of accountability, and organization analysis.

The Hay Plan is based on an interview between the job analyst and the job incumbent. The information that is gathered relates to four aspects of the incumbent's job: the objectives, the dimensions, the nature and scope of the position, and the accountability objectives. Information about the objectives allows the reader of the job description to know why the job exists in the organization and for what reason it is paid. Information about dimensions conveys to the reader how big a show the incumbent runs and the magnitude of the end results affected by his or her actions.

The real heart of the Hay Plan job description is the information about the nature and scope of the position, which covers five crucial aspects:

1. How the position fits into the organization, including reference to significant organizational and outside relationships.

2. The general composition of supporting staff. This includes a thumbnail sketch of each major function of any staff under the incumbent's position—size, type, and the reason for its existence.

3. The general nature of the technical, managerial, and human relations know-how required.

4. The nature of the problem solving required: What are the key problems that must be solved by this job, and how variable are they?

5. The nature and source of control on the freedom to solve problems and act, whether supervisory, procedural, or vocational or professional.

Information related to the accountability objectives tells what end results the job exists to achieve and the incumbent is held accountable for. There are four areas of accountability: organization (including staffing, developing, and maintaining the organization) and strategic planning, tactical planning, execution and directing the attainment of objectives, and review and control. Because the Hay Plan is based on information gathered in an interview (as opposed to the checklist method in the MPDQ, for example) the success of the Plan depends upon the skills of the interviewer. Interviewers can be trained, however. The Hay Plan continues to grow in popularity.

Functional Job Analysis (FJA) is another standardized approach. It was developed by the United States Training and Employment Service (USTES) to describe the nature of jobs and to develop job summaries, job descriptions, and employee specifications. FJA, originally meant to improve job placement and counseling for workers registering for employment at local employment offices, was part of an intensive research program directed toward producing the 1965 edition of the *Dictionary of Occupational Titles* (*DOT*). Today, many aspects of FJA are used by a number of private and public organizations.

FJA is both a conceptual system for defining the dimensions of worker activity and a method of measuring levels of worker activity. The basic premises of FJA are:

1. A fundamental distinction must be made between what gets done and what workers do to get things done. Bus drivers do not carry passengers; they drive vehicles and collect fares.

2. Jobs are concerned with data, people, and things.

3. In relation to things, workers draw on physical resources; in relation to data, on mental resources; and in relation to people, on interpersonal resources.

4. All jobs require the worker to relate to data, people, and things to some degree.

5. Although the behavior of workers or the tasks they perform can apparently be described in an infinite number of ways, there are only a few definitive functions involved. Thus, in interacting with machines, workers feed, tend, operate, and set up; in the case of vehicles or related machines, they drive or control them. Although these functions vary in difficulty and content, each draws on a relatively narrow and specific range of worker characteristics and qualifications for effective performance.

6. The functions appropriate to dealing with data, people, or things are hierarchical and ordinal, proceeding from the simple to the complex. Thus to indicate that a particular function, say compiling (data), reflects the requirements of a job is to say that it also includes the requirements of lower functions, such as comparing, and that it excludes the requirements of higher functions, such as analyzing.

The worker functions associated with data, people, and things are listed below. The USTES has used these worker functions as a basis for describing over 30,000 job titles in the *DOT*.

Functions Associated with Data, People, and Things

Data	People	Things
0 synthesizing	0 mentoring	0 setting up
1 coordinating	1 negotiating	1 precision working
2 analyzing	2 instructing	2 operating—controlling
3 compiling	3 supervising	3 driving—operating
4 computing	4 diverting	4 manipulating
5 copying	5 persuading	5 tending
6 comparing	6 speaking—signaling	6 feeding—offbearing
	7 serving	7 handling
	8 taking instructions—helping	

Work Logs

As with questionnaires and interviews, work log structure should be standardized to assure that gathered data from different employees is comparable (see Appendixes L and M for sample work logs). Work logs basically ask workers to keep a running record of what specific things they do on the job. If kept over an entire job cycle, these logs are an excellent way to gather detailed and accurate data on what and when work is accomplished. They are particularly useful for detecting the frequency or repetitiveness of different tasks. Questionnaires and interviews sometimes overlook certain key, but infrequently or randomly performed, tasks. A disadvantage is that employees can easily distort what they report for self-interest reasons.

Work logs are unpopular. Workers think they are disruptive, time consuming, and a general nuisance. The analyst must do a thorough sell job to get incumbents to accept the idea of doing a log and to get incumbents to do them consistently and accurately. Resistance can be minimized by pointing out the valuable insights logs can give workers into their own usage of time. Logs can really help workers become more efficient. Resistance can also be reduced by instructing the worker in how to fill out the logs. For example, log recordings need not be made after each individual act engaged in by the worker. Employees can usually wait until mid-morning, noon time, mid-afternoon, and the end of the workday to do their fill-ins for the time periods immediately preceding these points in time. Also workers should understand that very brief statements are usually all that are necessary to provide a clue as to what went on. Later on the analyst, during an interview perhaps, can fill in the details if necessary. Use of a precategorized task log such as in Appendix M can further reduce employee resistance because such an instrument requires essentially just a check mark to pinpoint the kind of task.

Direct (continuous) Observation

Direct observation of work is a valuable way to gather job data, especially when the worker is in a fixed location and is performing very observable tasks—that is, tasks other than think work, writing reports, and such. Assembly-line workers are a good example of a case where observation would pay off.

The analyst must be able to distinguish relevant acts (behavior) from irrelevant and be able to record accurately what is observed. The analyst must also take care not to interfere with the behavior of the worker. This is probably the greatest weakness of observation techniques. Of course the analyst must stay out of the way, but there is more to it than this. The presence of the observer usually distorts the performance of the worker unless the worker is fully and properly prepared for the observation scheme. Workers either slow down, speed up, or otherwise change their behavior to facilitate their self-interests. Some speed up to impress the analyst. Others slow down because they fear data will be used to set time standards or the like.

Generally, direct observation gives the most accurate and fullest indication of what a worker does. Other methods tend to provide data indirectly, which can be a great source of distortion, amplification, or filtration of the true picture. But direct observation is extremely expensive; it is the most time consuming of all methods if complete work cycles are to be observed.

Often observation on a limited basis is extremely worthwhile prior to using other techniques because it gives the analyst good insight into the boundaries of the job and, thereby, aides in interpreting log, interview, and questionnaire data.

Work Samples

Work sampling involves making instantaneous, random observations of what the worker is doing (see Appendix N for a sample random observation sheet used in taking work samples). If done properly, a fully accurate picture of what goes on can be derived at far less cost than with direct, continuous observation. Actually an observer can spot-check at random, a camera can be used to take snapshots at random intervals, or workers can be notified at random intervals to record what they are doing. With any of these approaches the essential data are acquired. A picture of how total time is distributed among work, non-work, and semi-work activities can be obtained over time. The keys are to make truly random observations (without forewarning the worker), and to make a sufficient number of observations over a complete work cycle.

Usually the analyst will select times, using a random number table or similar device, to observe the worker during each day over enough successive days to cover a work cycle. The analyst then has only to glance casually at the worker at each predetermined, selected time to determine what the worker is doing. A recording is made. This approach is fast, does not disrupt worker behavior, and is accurate. It obviously does not work well if the observer does not know where to find or how to contact the employee.

Filming

Films can be of great benefit when it is important not to miss a single task, when it is important to know precisely how long one spends on certain tasks, when a true picture of task detail is needed, or when information on task sequencing is required. Films are practical if the employee is relatively stationary in physical location since a camera can be positioned and left alone.

Films, of course, are not practical when employees move from location to location. They also can cause workers to operate abnormally because they either desire to impress the viewers or because they wish to build a case for changing certain parts of the job. Also films can be expensive to run over an extended period of time and expensive to review (because review takes considerable man-hours for the analyst). However, films are less expensive than direct observation because the analyst does not have to be there in person and can review the films during off hours.

Films are a superb tool for studying task detail because they can be slowed down, stopped, rewound, and replayed as often as is necessary to get an accurate task statement. They are also a superb tool for picking up unusual or unexpected events that tend to occur with some frequency but that data sources often forget to report by other means such as questionnaires and interviews. Films are better than direct observation because they do not rely on the analyst's interpretation and recording of tasks. Often analysts, though highly trained, are unfamiliar with jobs so sometimes they just do not know what should be recorded. The film is neither selective nor negligent in its recording.

Doing the Work Yourself

This is an excellent way to gather firsthand knowledge about a job. You can either do all the work yourself or serve in an apprentice or assistant role. This takes time and, therefore, is costly, but it gives the analyst a better real feel for the job than any other mechanism.

This method is workable when the job is easy to learn and is fairly structured. Complex jobs or jobs that involve considerable uncertainty in specific, day-to-day routines are really not amenable to this approach. It does not make sense to spend too much on training analysts to do a job they will perform only during the period of an analysis.

This method does make a lot of good sense when an organization finds itself faced with a type of job in which the details are left up to the incumbent. If the job involves a high degree of worker autonomy, involves relatively little interaction with others, is a one-of-a-kind role, and involves considerable movement from location to location, then there may be no other good way to gather accurate, valid data about the job. Each data-gathering data method has its place. The ones to choose will depend on many factors in the specific situation being addressed.

OTHER METHODS AND SOURCES

In addition to the major tools, analysts have at their disposal a wide range of other approaches for data gathering. One or more of these should usually be used in conjunction with a number of the major mechanisms just discussed.

Organization Charts, Process Charts, Layout Diagrams

Various charts and diagrams should be studied by any analyst prior to employment of other job data-gathering strategies because the understanding of the total organization provided by these devices will shape the nature of other strategies used and will help the analyst develop more worthwhile questions.

These charts and diagrams can provide insight into relationships among jobs—administrative and work relationships. They show flows of authority, of materials, of information. They can aid significantly in properly fitting a job into the overall structure of things. For example, if an organizational chart reveals a committee attached (authority-wise) to a particular position in the organization, this cues the analyst to find out who serves on that committee and to build that committee responsibility into the job descriptions of those who serve. Sometimes such responsibilities, which may not be highly time consuming and regular, are neglected by incumbents or supervisors providing job data.

Pocket Tape Recorders

Pocket tape recorders may be used in place of work logs. Incumbents can simply voice record what they are doing at different points in time. This may be less disruptive and less time consuming than stopping to fill in a work log sheet and thus may help to reduce resistance to keeping the log.

Such tape recorders can also be valuable to capture thoughts incumbents may have about their jobs while they are on the run without their questionnaires or work log sheets in hand. Later on, the worker can listen to the recorder and write down the important information. The problem with tape recorders is that you have to remember to turn them off and on. On occasion it may make sense just to leave the recorder on for a period of time during which there is a high volume of interpersonal interaction to capture a full vocal profile of what is happening on the job.

Pocket tape recorders are becoming more popular as a job analysis tool, but it does take time to listen to tapes and to record, in writing, what is heard on the tape. This is probably their major drawback.

Supervisor's Work Planning Notebooks

Good supervisors make work plans and keep these plans in some written form. Notebooks are frequently used for recording non-recurring as well as recurring delegated assignments with expected completion dates. Such notebooks, well kept, can provide one with a detailed and comprehensive view of many kinds of work engaged in by the employee. If delegated assignment completion dates are recorded in the notebook, insight can be gained into how long different tasks take. Such figures tend to be much more accurate than those supplied by workers during interviews or on questionnaires.

The supervisor's notebook can provide an excellent record of how one's job may be changing over time—changing in the kinds and volumes of assignments. It also will allow for ready analysis of work load distribution across all workers in the supervisor's department and may, thereby, suggest changes in job design to improve work load balance.

For jobs where a large percentage of the work is non-routine, highly random, or highly variable in nature, and delegated on a daily or weekly basis, the supervisor's notebook may be the very best source of objective data about work engaged in by the incumbent.

Daily To-do Lists and Appointment Books

If you can get employees to prepare and to save their to-do lists, you have another excellent source of information about what one does on the job (particularly when the to-do list is coupled with the supervisor's notebook). Getting employees to keep a to-do notebook with to-dos scheduled and crossed out as accomplished can provide very rich data on task sequences, required completion dates, work interruptions, uncertainty in task completion times, and such.

Properly kept appointment books can also provide valuable insight into the kinds of issues and problems the employee deals with, who else is involved, and when such issues were engaged. These books provide an objective, chronological record of certain work activities. For many jobs, they may serve in part as a substitute for keeping a work log. The appointment book is usually not seen as a nuisance as is the work log. Instead, it is viewed as an indispensable aid.

Critical Incidents Techniques

Critical incidents techniques can be powerful for establishing what is really important in a job. The approach is used in interviews or in questionnaires. Basically the incumbent is asked to identify key examples of job performance over the last six to twelve months that show real effectiveness or ineffectiveness. Or incumbents may be asked to list six to twelve things they must be good at in order to do the job well. The analyst will then probe these areas to identify key task domains, duties within each domain, task frequency, time consumption, and importance.

A variation of this approach is to ask incumbents to categorize their job into six to fifteen or so major responsibility domains. After this, incumbents are asked to identify specific duties within each domain, how long duties take, how important they are, what skills and abilities are essential in each domain, what resources are used to carry out duties, and when duties are performed. The primary point in these approaches is to structure and stimulate incumbent thinking about the job by first having incumbents focus on critical, or major, aspects of performance on the job. This cues the analyst on what to pursue in probing for data.

Communication Records

Almost any written communication associated with a job—any information related to the job or its performance written by the jobholder or sent to the jobholder—can give insight into characteristics of the job. It may take time to analyze paperwork associated with a job and it may be difficult to convert information from this source to worthwhile statements of responsibility, but such an approach tends to be objective and uncovers task items otherwise missed.

Interoffice memos, file drawers, bulletin boards, telephone log books, records of office visits, routing slips, mail, travel records, progress reports, and even the content of waste baskets can provide valuable clues of what and when the employee performs. Just studying what is on top of one's desk or what information is stored in one's work area can yield worthwhile insights.

Former Employees

Former employees often see little advantage to be gained by distorting the picture of their old jobs, so this is a good way to avoid bias in reporting. Present employees often do see an advantage in this. You can use interviews or questionnaires with former employees. Some combination is probably best. A good practice is to make the exit interview, in part, a job analysis session. You do not want to wait too long to gather data from former employees because you lose touch with them. Jobs change after people leave and people cannot remember.

Some companies use exit interviews with good-performing retiring employees as the primary source of job data. These interviews do not disrupt the performance of a present employee and usually provide data from one with considerable experience and understanding of the true nature of the job. The disadvantage here is that by not involving the present incumbent you miss an opportunity for the worker to gain understanding and insight into the job through participation in the process of generating and compiling data about the job. One of the great advantages of using work logs, interviews, and questionnaires is not so much the data itself generated but the learning that it provides the worker. New supervisors, for example, can benefit immensely from participation in a job analysis exercise.

Old JDs and JDs of Other Similar Jobs

Do not reinvent the wheel every time you are faced with the task of preparing a job description. Often old JDs will exist. They may be grossly out of date and out of touch with reality, but they can still provide valuable data or suggestions on where to focus a job analysis study. Job descriptions used in other parts of the organization for similar jobs can prove valuable for helping one structure and write a JD as well as for suggesting what kinds of responsibilities/duties to investigate and ask questions about. Also getting copies of JDs used in other organizations for similar types of work can save a great deal of time by suggesting desirable formats, writing style, task statement content, and so forth.

Professional groups, associations, and agencies often have JDs on file for jobs that are fairly standard in an industry. A medical lab technician in one hospital, for example, is likely to have essentially the same job as a medical lab tech in another hospital. Acquiring JDs from other organizations engaged in the same kind of production/service as yours can significantly help in reducing the burden of JD preparation in your company.

Panels of Experts

There can be great advantages in using groups to provide job data. The comments of one member will provide feed for others and a fuller picture of a job will emerge. Also a more accurate picture will emerge as inaccurate or inappropriate data will likely be caught and screened out when a number of people are discussing a job's content.

Crucial here is to get experts on your panel—perhaps employees who now supervise but at one time worked in the job being studied, personnel specialists, competent experienced workers who at one time held the job under consideration or who have related to the job frequently over the years, or perhaps workers on job rotation who have experienced the job as well as other related jobs and, therefore, understand how the job fits into the system. Outsiders who have backgrounds related to the job or who work at similar jobs in other companies can also be used. Assembling panels of experts can be costly, but you do get objectivity. You have to be careful to assemble people with true knowledge of the job, however. This may be difficult because if they do not do the job or do not directly supervise, the question can be raised: "Just how much do they really know about the job?"

Budgets and Expense Records

Budgets, together with records of actual expenditures, can provide insight into the nature of work because they show what money is spent for—what resources are purchased to work with. Each item purchased by a company should be used in some way to accomplish some kind of work. Reviewing budgets and expenditure records may stimulate the analyst to develop certain lines of questioning about duties ignored or forgotten, with other job analysis approaches. For example, the analyst may discover an unusual piece of equipment rented during a particular time of year. This leads to questions about what it was used for, who used it, how much time was spent with it, what specific tasks did workers have relative to this equipment, and so on. Knowledge of this unusual event can perhaps stimulate considerable insight into what turns out to be time-consuming but unplanned work—something that should be acknowledged in a JD.

Work Plans

Various types of work plans such as organizational and departmental objectives, production schedules, work orders, methods annuals, and written procedures can cue the analyst on certain areas to probe. The analyst can find out just what parts of these plans the incumbent is involved with.

Often rather comprehensive sets of work objectives are prepared for individual jobs or positions. These certainly can provide rich data on what the job is like. The conversion from objectives to statements of duties, or tasks, is not usually a difficult one.

Performance evaluation instruments and objectives, though usually prepared after job descriptions are prepared, are frequently prepared apart from the existence of any job descriptions. When this is done, these documents can provide a wealth of insight for preparation of the JD. They usually spell out key areas in which the incumbent is supposed to perform well. Keep in mind, however, that this is working backward. It is more appropriate to design and describe the job first, then to decide the criteria and objectives to be used to evaluate worker performance.

Management Committees and Groups of Workers

Committees and groups may not be experts as discussed in "Panels of Experts" above, but groups do generate a variety of ideas and perspectives and tend to generate valid data as mentioned earlier. Biases get screened out. Having a management committee develop data for job descriptions across the organization helps assure standardization in data acquisition procedures and in the format and content of prepared JDs. Using management committees can also help distribute the burden of gathering and assembling data and it serves to place the burden of designing jobs and preparing JDs where it probably should be—on a management team.

Activity Matrix

The activity matrix approach is a special way of getting employees to think about their jobs in terms of (a) various major functions they perform, (b) products or services they produce, (c) physical location at which they work, and/or (d) types of customers they relate to. Incumbents are requested to record time spent relative to each category and to list people, data, and things they come into contact with in each of the subcategories identified under each category. Duty statements with time percentages are then formulated.

NOTES

1. The section of additional hints for preparing and using questionnaires is adapted from Michael R. Carrell and Frank E. Kuzmits, *Personnel* (Columbus, Ohio: Charles E Merrill, 1982), p. 83.

2. The section on standardized questionnaires, checklists, and FJAs is adapted from Randall S. Schuler, *Personnel and Human Resource Management* (St. Paul, Minn.: West Publishing, 1987), pp. 102-7.

CHAPTER 5

The Most Common Problems with Job Descriptions

This chapter will, in part, serve to summarize key points made earlier. In practice, considerable problems exist with respect to JD use and preparation. They are neither used properly nor nearly as fully as they could be. They are neither written properly nor based on quality data. By addressing the kinds of problems highlighted here, organizations can considerably improve their management of the human resource. Most of these problems are rather easily surmounted. Primarily what is required is simple awareness of their existence. So many problems associated with JDs exist but are not recognized by anyone and, therefore, go unattended.

It is likely to be difficult for an organization, however, to resolve these problems without a coordinated effort. One office in the organization—whether it be a large or small organization—should be charged with the responsibility and given the authority necessary to take action on these problems across all organizational levels and departments. JD preparation and use is no more or less important in one part of the company than in another, so an organization-wide thrust should be made.

THE WRITTEN DOCUMENT

Job descriptions typically are not prepared very well. Because of this their great potential usefulness is seldom fully realized. The following items should make clear to the reader just what the most common deficiencies are and should, therefore, help writers of job descriptions improve their work:

Not up-to-date. Companies are notorious for letting job descriptions sit in the file without periodic review and updating. Jobs must change to accommodate new technologies, growth of the employee, new customer requirements—and so should the JDs that describe those jobs. Indeed, JD revision should facilitate job redesign and should, therefore, *lead* job design change, not lag behind. An out-of-date JD is not just useless, it is dangerous if managers attempt to use it in some of the important areas discussed in Chapter 2. An out-of-date JD is an inaccurate JD and can only lead to error in management of the human resource. JDs should be updated annually or semi-annually in association with employee performance reviews, or a system should be devised that assures job change information is channeled to those responsible for updating JDs as changes in jobs are made.

Not standardized in format across departments. Nothing is more frustrating to a new manager looking at JDs in the company for the first time—perhaps to help determine needed adjustments in pay—than discovering that each JD for each position in his or her department is structured differently or that job descriptions in departments in his or her area of authority are structured totally differently from JDs in other departments. Such a state of affairs makes it next to impossible to compare jobs. Equitable pay cannot be established. Proper work load balance cannot be achieved. Proper employee selection techniques cannot be devised if JDs for different positions do not have the same basic structure. The formulation of JDs in a company should be coordinated by one analyst, by the personnel department, or by a management committee to assure standardization. Managers must not be allowed to invent their own personal preference JDs.

Incomplete and too general. A number of managers say they prefer JDs that are not too long and lacking in detail and specifics. The reason: Such JDs do not tie them down to a rigid contractual arrangement. But the JD that is not comprehensive, sufficiently detailed, and written with precise, specific statements is a relatively useless instrument. What the job design really is like is left largely to guess.

The perceived rigid contractual arrangement problem can be easily avoided by indicating in the JD an "Other" work category. Such a category points out that all duties cannot be planned in advance—some things (perhaps many) have to be done rather spontaneously and it is, therefore, a must that organizations keep flexible and be able to change jobs as demand dictates.

By preparing a detailed and complete JD, important aspects of the job are not neglected. This is a vital consideration when using the JD to orient and train new workers, for example, or to guide the redesign of work.

There is never any excuse for vague, unclear, general statements in the JD. Such statements only confuse the reader, allow for personalized interpretation of the job, and consequently lead to improper performance. A number of people should check the wording of proposed JDs to assure clarity and precision in language.

Lacking duty categories. JDs that incorporate, say, forty duty statements without any arrangement or grouping patterns are confusing and fail to provide the reader any real direction or insight into the basic rationale for the job. Interpretation of the nature of the job—its key components and priorities—is aided by categorizing responsibilities in some way: by function, by work location, by time of execution, or whatever. This allows the reader to separate the trees from the forest and prevents the worker from losing sight of important overall job dimensions. It is like reading a textbook. Would you want to read 500 pages with no chapters, headings, or subheadings?

No task time and priority data. JDs are frequently assembled without attention given to the relative importance of different duties and the relative time consumption of different duties. Leaving out such information misleads the reader of the JD. All duties appear equal. On every job some tasks are important and some not so important. These differences are vital to recognize when evaluating employee performance, for example, or when hiring workers. Also, on every job some duties take longer than others. This is essential to recognize in designing jobs for proper work load, task variety, and so on. It is a rather simple matter to add priority and time consumption data to JDs. Workers usually have these things rather clearly in mind so job analysis techniques can easily elicit such data.

Key general responsibilities left out. Often JDs neglect to incorporate reference to key duties or responsibilities, which apply across the entire work force or, at least, across a large segment of it. These are the things all workers are expected to do, such as fill out time cards, prepare for the annual performance review, visit with guests touring the plant, and annually update their own JDs. JDs are often excessively focused on the unique aspects of a job—on how the job differs from others. This is fine for many purposes but really does not show the true job design. True work loads, for example, are not indicated. Also the JD is not particularly useful for such matters as new employee orientation if the responsibilities common to all workers are left out.

Not position specific. It was just stated that JDs fail to cover general responsibilities that apply across many workers. But it is perhaps even more common and more of a problem when JDs do not reflect adequately the uniqueness of each different position. Often companies try to write one JD to cover all workers doing essentially the same kind of work. But such an approach may miss vital, though subtle differences. For example, different department heads in an organization may have essentially the same types of major responsibilities, but specific duties, time spent on various areas, and task priorities may differ substantially from one manager to the next. One department manager may be loaded with routine and planned work, while others spend more time with spontaneous execution and troubleshooting. JDs should reflect the unique character of each position and not attempt to cover too many different positions. If this is not done the JD does not accurately reflect the actual work design.

Too often descriptive rather than prescriptive. JDs are frequently prepared after the fact—after the work is designed—and are prepared largely with data submitted from the incumbent. The result: a picture of what *is*, rather than what *should* be. Managers at all levels must get involved in JD preparation to control design and to assure that the work done is what is in the best interest of the organization. JDs should prescribe what ought to happen. Periodic performance reviews should compare what does happen with what ought to, and should lead to adjustments when discrepancies are found. Too often companies let jobs evolve into "products of the incumbent"—jobs compatible with incumbent interests rather than with organizational interests.

Confusingly mixed with performance standards, person specs, and/or rules and regulations. Many so-called job descriptions attempt to incorporate performance-level expectations—quantity, quality, timeliness, and cost criteria—with defined standards of performance. Some companies have adopted these results-oriented descriptions in an attempt to improve the value of their JDs. But performance criteria—ways of measuring—are not part of the design of the job and are, therefore, best left for a separate performance evaluation instrument—perhaps attached to the JD but distinct from it.

Extremely common is the practice of including personal qualifications and required abilities, skills, and knowledge—person specs—in the JD (see Appendix B). These are vital for getting the right people for jobs but they are descriptions of the kind of person needed for the job, not descriptions of the job. Again, there may be considerable merit in attaching person specs to the JD, but the distinction between the job description and person specs should be clear. They are not the same thing.

A relatively recent trend that adds to the confusion is incorporation in the job description of skills, knowledge, and abilities that one should become proficient at while on the job. This practice has a worthwhile objective—to show incumbents or prospective workers how they can expect to progress (develop) while on the job, which helps in plotting job change trajectories—but such information should not be crammed into the JD. A separate document—again attached, if you like, to the JD—makes things clearer.

Often rules and regulations get mixed in with duty statements. The author recently reviewed JDs that incorporated required safe work practices in lists of duties. Statements like "Avoids carrying two acid-filled beakers at once" or "Wears hard hat when doing warehouse stacking" are not really statements of work to be done. However, a statement like "Checks floor daily to assure not slippery" may be a legitimate duty statement. Admittedly, it can be difficult to show the appropriate line between what should go in the JD and what would be better left for a separate document.

Temporary work left out. Most jobs will have temporary assignments built in from time to time. Special projects, committee assignments, and one-time tasks, for example, may have to be delegated to employees. Any duty planned in advance for execution over a year or less duration should go in the JD in a special Temporary Assignment section. It is a fully legitimate part of the design of the job. Not acknowledging such work (which is a frequent occurrence) leads to flaws in end-of-year performance evaluation, work load assessments, and so on. A good practice is to add each year—perhaps during the performance review—a Temporary Assignment section to the JD. This section makes it a dynamic document. Recognizing how essential temporary activity engagement is and accepting the practice of acknowledging it in the JD stimulates that all-important periodic review of the job description.

Do not show how non-task time is spent. Amazingly, if you add up the time percentages associated with duty statements in many a JD, you get 100 percent. This, you know, cannot be right. No worker ever spent 100 percent of his or her on-the-job day doing work. Managers and operative employees are idle waiting for delays, taking breaks, socializing at work, and engaging in semi-work activities such as in-plant or out-of-plant travel. JDs should recognize how one's time is truly spent by indicating time allotment to these non-work and semi-work engagements. On some jobs these are significant time-consuming categories. Failure to acknowledge them in the JD highly misrepresents the design of the work.

Tell what but not where, when, how often, with whom, and under what conditions. Most traditional JDs tell what the worker does. Left out are descriptions of where, when, frequency, who else is involved, and conditions under which the work is performed. A full picture of work is missing without these additional data. What good is a statement that says, "Files documents" if left out is the fact that this is done only six times a year, at the beginning of odd numbered months in six different cities with help from forty assistants?

Likewise, leaving out definitions of the conditions under which work is performed can be misleading. Two persons' JDs may say, "Files documents" but one of these people may perform this task in a physically cold, socially isolated environment under very little pressure. The other person may have an extremely demanding filing task—expected to file as many as thirty legal documents within a five-minute time span, every hour, in a busy office, while the telephone is constantly ringing.

Do not indicate kinds of decisions incumbent can make. JDs usually leave out discussions of the independent authority that can be exercised by the jobholder. What kinds of decisions can the incumbent make without checking with higher authority? Who *must* be consulted in decision making? Whose advice *must* be sought prior to decision making? Can certain decisions be made independently or must they be a product of group effort? For example, will the employee be permitted to fire a subordinate without input from others? Will an employee be permitted to spend $5,000 on a piece of equipment without input from others? Will whether or not the employee can exercise independent judgment be a product of his or her experience or past performance record? These kinds of issues should be clarified in the JD.

Duties hidden in a narrative format. In today's organizations the narrative-type JD has little place. These JDs camouflage the work. Precise enumeration of duties is far superior. Listing duty statements shows how the work is divided up. It shows the distinctive components of the work. It clearly helps one detect the volume and variety of work activities. The narrative approach, though sometimes tending to provide better conceptual integration of the various parts of the job, tends to hinder real study and analysis of the job's structure and design. The narrative approach does not give each job dimension clear identity. The best way is to sum up the entire job with a general-function paragraph near the beginning of the document but avoid narratives for sub-function description.

Functional authority and staff authority linkages unclear. JDs usually indicate superior and subordinate line positions relative to a given job but seldom clearly define other key administrative links—those of a functional or staff authority nature. So often in organizations employees do, in fact, receive or give orders to people outside the chain of command. This is often done for years without formal definition or authorization. All is well as long as the employees involved are highly experienced people who have learned, and accepted, the system. But with high turnover in an organization—new people frequently starting up on the job—failure to delineate functional and staff authority connections can lead to months, if not years, of conflict, frustration, and employee abuse.

No job family or career ladder data. It is most useful if employees understand, up front, how their jobs fit in to the total system in terms of providing opportunities for job change and advancement. What *other* jobs are similar, requiring similar skills, or requiring development of the same base skills learned on the job being described? Indicating job families and career tracks gives workers a fuller perspective of their work (thus helping them to better understand their places in the organization), helps workers prepare for other positions, and shows workers with whom they ought to consult for advice about their present jobs. It is vital information, legitimately placed in the JD because it shows the design of the larger system of which a particular position is a part.

Not dated and signed by the proper people. As with any other valuable document, when you pull it from the file drawer you want to know when it was prepared and who was responsible for its preparation and/or who approved it. No different with job descriptions; but many an on-file JD can be found with no preparation date, no indication of when it was last reviewed/revised, and no signatures of the incumbent, the supervisor, the preparer of the JD, or of the person who ok'd the JD's content. You look at it and wonder if it was prepared last year or five years ago, and if it was ever authorized by anyone. There can be no excuse for lack of dates and signatures.

Excessive redundancy and overloaded with non-job design data. Some JDs confuse the design of the work by saying the same thing, or almost the same thing, in different ways in different task statements. This confuses the design and makes the job appear far more complex than it is. Care must be taken to write duty statements that are mutually exclusive or non-overlapping.

A further common problem is the tendency of some preparers of JDs to build too much data into the JD. Comprehensiveness is essential and sufficient detail is important, but any data such as descriptions of methods, work objectives, or discussion of informal roles should be left for other documents. Do not abuse the JD by encompassing non-job design data.

No recognition of unplanned work. Much of the typical employee's job will involve unplanned, spur-of-the-moment assignments, self-initiatives, and so on. Random, unpredictable demands can occupy a major portion of one's time on management-type jobs. The typical JD does not recognize this category of activity. To get a clear sense of the design of the work, this category should be incorporated into the JD. Not doing this means the JD will be highly misleading as an accurate descriptor of the job's design.

USE OF THE DOCUMENT

Even well-written JDs are highly underutilized and misused in practice. There are numerous reasons for this, all of which can be constructively addressed and minimized if not eliminated. The following pinpoints common specific problems in the use (or non-use) of job descriptions:

Not used because of lack of understanding about how to use. Perhaps the most widespread problem with the usage of JDs is that managers do not know how, or for what purposes, to use them. Most managers have never been trained on how to interpret JDs, let alone on how to prepare them and for what to use them. Few managers can give you more than six or eight uses for job descriptions—far short of the 132 uses identified in Chapter 2. If managers are to put this powerful document to work, they must receive some training—training that covers how to gather data for JDs and how to prepare them as well as how to use them. Without this, the potential utility of JDs will never be very fully realized.

Not used because perceived as inflexible contract. Many managers and subordinates see JDs as a work contract spelling out exactly what the worker will do—no more, no less. Managers see JDs, therefore, as imposing a constraint on how the human resource will be used. They see JDs as rigidifying job content, thereby interfering with the frequent need to adapt jobs to different workers and to changing conditions, and to delegate different kinds of tasks from time to time. Workers use them as an excuse not to change or adapt. The JD thus causes a degree of resistance to change.

JDs should not be viewed as limiting change or as restricting what can be delegated. JDs should be written with an "Other" category built in to allow for different kinds of assignments and should be viewed as something that needs regular updating either as a stimulus for change or in response to work changes. After all, the JD is but a piece of paper. It does not control; managers control.

Not used for fear they are ill-prepared or out-of-date. Often managers do not bother with JDs in the file because of the feeling (often not fact) that those JDs were not very well prepared in the first place. Perhaps the manager senses that the person responsible for preparation of the JD lacked expertise or has heard about specific flaws in the data used to compile the JDs. If one does not have confidence in the validity of the JD, one is unlikely to use it. Similarly, managers often are aware that the JDs for jobs in their areas have not been reviewed and updated for months or years. Using out-of-date documents—with irrelevant content—just leads to shoddy management. Best not to use them at all is the thinking. Companies must develop procedures to make sure JDs are prepared by people skilled in such preparation and that JDs are kept up-to-date.

Not used because of perception that the job escapes definition. Many jobs have an uncertain content. You can seldom be sure just what the worker will have to spend time doing. The assistant-to-the-president-type job is a case in point. Other jobs, though having stable, definable content for given periods of time, change dramatically in content from one time period to the next—and these time periods may be relatively short. Still other jobs involve an extremely great variety of tasks—like the job of a handyman. Under such circumstances managers often see little sense in using job descriptions because they think that the JDs cannot possibly reflect reality. The descriptions would be too long, changed too often, or necessarily vague.

Quality JDs can be written to accommodate such circumstances and with properly developed procedures can be adjusted frequently at very low cost. Task categorizing can be used to prevent excessive numbers of tasks from having to be listed in the JD. Frequent changing of JDs is not difficult once a basic JD format is developed and a standard procedure is in place for giving attention to JD change as job design is changed. Jobs with uncertain content can be treated as a probabilistic system—identifying task distributions—or can be described by simply acknowledging the uncertain portion with the category "Other" and attaching an approximate time percentage and priority to it.

Not used because of perception JDs should not be built around the individual. Organizations will want to adapt jobs to incumbent strengths and weaknesses. Perhaps certain duties should be eliminated from one's job and assigned elsewhere if these duties, for one reason or another, cannot be performed proficiently by the worker. Perhaps the worker should be assigned other tasks, not normally part of the job, to take advantage of special skills or knowledge he or she has. Also, as the employee grows in the job, job content should evolve to take advantage of the increased capacity of the worker. Jobs are, in part, what people make them—what workers make them.

Recognizing this, some managers feel job descriptions are not appropriate and of little value because they must reflect the character of the incumbent. The content of a job, so goes the argument, is not independent of the particular individual doing the job. This argument continues, pointing out that jobs are built around people. People are not molded to fit jobs. Actually, there is a strong element of truth here. But most of what the employee will do for the organization will be based on organizational need, not on personal need. If jobs were largely products of the individual personality, organizations would soon be out of control. JDs show the necessary organizational need encompassed by jobs—and that end they serve well.

Misused as a substitute for job evaluation instrumentation. Job descriptions are vital for comparing jobs and establishing fair base wages/salaries, but they are not a substitute for a job factor sheet (see Appendix O). To develop wage/salary equity a job factor sheet must be developed and then JDs used to determine, from the factor sheet, relative job worths, or scores. The nature of the job and its requirements as depicted by the JD (and person specs) can be assessed and valued by the factor sheet. The JD alone does not permit ease of determining job worth. Determining job worth for pay or other purposes requires a fully developed factor scoring system.

Misused as a substitute for person specs. Appendix B shows a set of person specs; Appendix A shows a job description. Person specs tell what kind of *person* is required on the job. These are derived from an analysis of required duties and responsibilities in the JD and are necessary for recruiting, selecting, and training. Managers often err in using JDs directly in recruiting, selecting, and training. You can use JDs directly, certainly, but a much better job of recruiting, selecting, and training can be done if managers go one step beyond the JD and infer a set of person specs with required ability, skill, and knowledge levels clearly defined and put in writing. JDs are too infrequently used for derivation of person spec documents—too often used as a substitute for person specs.

Misused as a substitute for a performance assessment instrument. Appendix D shows a performance evaluation instrument. JDs alone are of little value for measuring performance. They tell what areas to look at in evaluating performance but not *how* to measure it. Often managers will use JDs to pinpoint the kinds of things on which employees should be evaluated, but as a performance assessment tool this is the limit of the JD. Performance assessment done directly with the JD is necessarily a highly subjective affair. One must devise quantity, quality, timeliness, and cost measures (criteria) of each task dimension in the JD and set standards, or desired levels of performance, along each criterion before performance can be assessed. As with person specs, development of performance criteria and standards is one step beyond the JD.

Not used consistently by, and uniformly across, departments. If JDs are successfully used for hiring purposes in March, why are they not used in October? If they significantly contribute to proper employee orientation in the production department, why are they not used in engineering? These are legitimate questions that every organization ought to be asking itself. Because JD usage is usually not planned well in advance and coordinated throughout the organization, inconsistency in usage and lack of uniform usage are commonly rampant.

Someone, or some department—the personnel department if an organization has one—should assure that the value of JDs is realized on a consistent basis throughout the organization. On-again, off-again use, coupled with one use here, some other use there, is representative of neglect of a vital tool. JD potential can only be fully realized by organizations that make a steady, long-term, company-wide, uniform effort at using them.

Not used because of lack of sufficient detail or usable content. Many managers say they want JDs prepared but they never use them because they are too general and really say little about what the incumbent actually does. Precision and detail are absolutely essential if proper orientation, training, and performance assessment instrument design are to come from them. Also managers complain that their JDs are not valuable and, therefore, not used because the content is not relevant to their purposes. The manager may wish to study resources used on the job, but the JDs do not mention these. Or the manager may wish to study a job for detection of low-time-consuming task items that might possibly be assigned elsewhere, but the JD does not contain task time percentages.

Not used to motivate and lead. One of the most powerful uses of JDs is to lead and motivate workers, but this is one of the most infrequent uses of JDs. JDs give workers direction. They make things clear to the incumbent like how much effort should be distributed across different duties, how much attention should be given to different duties to assure their accurate completion, and so on. Bosses do not need to be around all the time to provide face-to-face leadership and motivation. Much of this can come from the JD. If JDs are prepared properly and distributed to workers, workers need only refer to them to obtain much needed information on performance expectations. The clearer the performance expectations, the more motivated one will be.

Not prepared for all employees. All employees should have JDs. They are just as useful (and feasible) for top-level managers as for rank and file employees; but many organizations do not have JDs for certain professional people and high-level managers. Lack of JDs means considerable loss of control of worker behavior and performance. Also when some departments have JDs for their people and others do not, the JDs in those departments that do have them are rendered less useful because, for example, opportunities for comparing jobs across departments are reduced. Further, having JDs for some employees and not others raises serious questions about ethics and preferential treatment.

Not fully communicated to employees. Some companies have quality JDs but they do not tell anyone—not even the workers themselves. Some companies keep JDs a secret—filed away somewhere, in a rather inaccessible personnel office file. Obviously it does little good to invest in JD preparation if JDs are not communicated to employees and their supervisors. Why do companies do this? Usually it is simply because of failure to recognize the utility of the well-prepared JD when placed in the hands of employees and supervisors. Sometimes it is because managers feel they have greater power over workers if they alone know what the job is really like. Keeping the worker in the dark is a social power strategy preferred by more supervisors than they care to admit.

Use is too mechanical. Some companies, often those that rely on personnel departments for management of the human resource, do not look beyond the JD in human resource management (HRM). They blindly apply the JD in HRM. They assume the JD tells all about a job—or at least all that is important—but this assumption is frequently faulty. JDs are best used by the experienced supervisor who knows full well what the JD is not telling him or her as well as what it is.

JDs have to be applied with an open mind and flexible attitude. For example, if a candidate for a job seems to lack experience in two vital areas of responsibility, mechanical use of the JD might suggest the candidate be dropped from employment consideration. However, the professional user of a JD will look at other factors. Perhaps this candidate has an extremely positive attitude that would be valuable as a stimulus to others in the particular work group of which he or she would be a member. Perhaps the candidate has something in his or her background, like continued arrests for stealing, that should be considered in matching a person to a job but that would not be brought out by strict adherence to job descriptions and associated person specs.

Not used for enforcement of work that needs to be done. Employees naturally gravitate toward pursuit of self-interests while at work and toward expenditure of effort and time on the more desirable tasks. This tendency often leads to misdirected effort (from the company's point of view) in a fairly short time if someone is not watching. Managers neglect to use JDs to periodically monitor how the workers are spending their time and whether or not that time is being spent on coverage of *all* essential tasks. Mid-level managers and higher-ups are notorious for neglecting many a small, uninteresting, but nonetheless important task and no one ever catches it until it is too late. Someone must assure that what is in the JDs *is* done. If it does not have to be done, get it out of the JD.

Not used because of lack of format comparability from department to department. If JDs are not standardized in format across departments, their utility is severely diminished. But many companies do not coordinate JD preparation across departments; they leave it up to individual supervisors. The result is a hodgepodge of styles, structure, and content. Jobs in one area cannot be compared with jobs in another. Quality and consistent structure in person specs, performance evaluation instruments, and job factor sheets can, therefore, not be obtained. Rather than use such JDs, they are ignored and efforts, independent of consideration of the JDs, are made to develop person specs, performance evaluation instruments, and job factor sheets. A company should have an organization-wide policy to help control and coordinate JD preparation and use.

JDs are not adhered to. Many companies have JDs but seem to disregard them. Jobs soon come to look nothing like what the JD says, as exceptions are always made to the assigned set of tasks specified in the JD. Managers often say they need flexibility in work assignments—true enough. But repeated catapulting over the boundaries of the JD may soon mean employee abuse. One of the reasons for JDs is to provide some sort of parameter within which the employee is expected to function. This motivates the employee and allows for better control of employee functioning in the organization. Repeated, excessive violation of the JD renders it a far less important tool for managing performance.

Not used because of perception that they are too much of a constraint on hiring. A number of managers disregard job descriptions in hiring. They say that what they are looking for is a candidate with the right attitude, a willingness to learn, and an aptitude for the work. Experience and developed skill relative to particular duties are not important. Besides, the intent is to mold the job to fit the individual's unique talents anyway. These managers see JDs as providing too narrow a profile of who might be acceptable to hire. They also often feel that what is needed is an employee who can constantly contribute beyond any formal job description—an employee who not only fulfills his or her own role, but who also shares and helps others fulfill their roles.

Even in this case the JD has a key role to play—not as a definitive portrayal of the work to be done, but as a guideline and approximation to the work to be done. No one says you cannot consider other factors like motivation, attitude, or aptitude that may not be spelled out in the JD or person specs but that anyone knows are related to performance. JDs must be viewed for what they are—*aids* to human resource decision making, not *substitutes* for decision making or inflexible *constraints* on decision making.

Not all displayed in one publication. Many managers—particularly divisional or upper level managers—have been frustrated to learn that all the organization's JDs cannot be found in one bound volume. To study work patterns in an organization and to determine things like possible redepartmentalization or repartitioning of work, it is extremely handy to have all job descriptions arranged systematically in one place. Usually, however, an analyst will have to spend a considerable amount of time gathering together JDs from different places before study can begin. Even an organization without a personnel department and without a person or group coordinating the preparation of JDs could easily arrange to have all JDs assembled in one manual. One person in an organization should have the responsibility of seeing to it that this is done. This allows for quick reference to any job at any level in the organization and allows the analyst to review JDs as parts of an integrated system.

Neglected during employee orientations. No document or reference literature is more valuable to any new employee than is the JD. A copy of the JD should be given to the new employee early on during orientation. Discussion and clarification of the components of the job, as highlighted in the JD, is at the heart of any orientation. But companies fail to do this—sometimes because of fear of overwhelming the employee, sometimes because those conducting the orientation are themselves unfamiliar with the content of the JD, and sometimes because managers do not want to lock in new persons until they have demonstrated what they can or cannot do. These are weak arguments compared with the great advantage of JD usage in orientation—clarifying job expectations.

No motivation for supervisors to use. Supervisors often ignore JDs not only because they are not trained to use them but also because there is no inducement to use them. Their managers do not use them and do not encourage their use. Annual evaluations of performance never involve discussion of JD use. When bonuses come out, no supervisor gets rewarded for effective use of JDs. JDs can help managers be better managers but JDs are a means to an end. They often are ignored in debates about performance. Managers get rewarded for results—bottom lines. Though JDs properly utilized can help achieve a favorable bottom line, they are usually overlooked as a key contributing factor. Managers are almost never directly rewarded for their effective use. Focusing rewards only on results is often a mistake.

GATHERING DATA FOR THE DOCUMENT

A job description is only as good as the quality of the data collected to write it. Many a JD is written well—right "by the book" as far as what information is included and how it is presented; but the validity of the information is suspect. The JD is not based on properly acquired data. In the following, specific common problems with gathering data are highlighted:

Data distorted for self-interest. One of the most significant problems in job analysis is getting unbiased data—data truly reflective of the normal work routine. Good data are hard to come by whether you are using observation techniques, self-reporting techniques, or interviews. The natural tendency is for incumbents to distort the pictures they give of their jobs for self-serving purposes. Some will want to impress the analyst, thinking that somehow such will benefit them in the long run. It is quite common for incumbents to inflate how much work they do, the variety of demands placed on them, and the importance of the decisions they make. Some employees may sense that the data being gathered are going to be used to set output standards or to expand the content of their jobs so they slow down and make sure they fill up their day with relatively few but time-consuming tasks. Others will have some special point they wish to make and they will see the job analysis as a way to influence management by assuring this special point gets recorded in the data. The author knows one employee who inflated the number of telephone calls he received in a given day so that he could get his own telephone for *his* desk.

To guard against this kind of distorted data, it is important to gather data by multiple means from multiple sources so checks and balances exist on what is received for data. Also, incumbents must be thoroughly schooled and motivated to provide truthful data. This may require extensive orientation about the analysis. These points are elaborated on in the next three paragraphs.

Subjects not motivated and trained to provide data. Too often job analyses falsely assume that incumbents can and will provide data automatically—all you have to do is request it. Nothing could be further from the truth. Most workers do not know what a job analysis is and have little sense of its value or why the company is doing one. As with anything else, if you want workers to perform well they must be fully motivated and trained. They have to be instructed in how to fill out questionnaires, work logs, and such, and have to be intensely aware of how such information is going to be of value to them and the company. Employees will resist job analysis exercises if not fully prepared for them and if they do not fully believe in them. It is up to management to place a high priority on these exercises, communicate this to the workers, and assure that the workers have time to fit data providing into their work routines.

One method too often used for data acquisition. This is an extremely common flaw in data gathering. Many companies rely solely on gathering data by questionnaire. This is a quick method and assures standardization in what is acquired, but standing alone it, as well as any other method used alone, will not provide the variety and depth of perspective one needs to prepare a quality job description. Other methods need to be used to elicit data that cannot be gathered well with the questionnaire, such as real feelings about the importance of certain aspects of work or recurring problems encountered at work. Also, other methods, such as the interview, need to be used to provide more detailed and elaborate descriptions of work as well as verification of data.

Excessive reliance on one source of data. Some companies rely almost exclusively on self-reporting of work by the incumbent. Other companies have only the supervisor provide data on jobs. Still others place the burden almost entirely on specialists in the personnel department who are highly trained in continuous or work-sampling observation techniques. But again, checks and balances on data gathered need to be developed and using multiple sources is one way to do this. Incumbents, peers, supervisors, personnel specialists, and the incumbent's subordinates can all offer useful data about the incumbent's job. A team approach here is valuable. It is usually an absolute must to collect job information from at least the incumbent and his or her supervisor. Incumbents know what *is* done; supervisors know what *should be* done. Ironing out any differences here can be a valuable developmental process for both incumbent and supervisor.

Prefab instrumentation. There are many advocates of using standardized questionnaires for job analysis such as PAQ and MPDQ. But these instruments are not well adapted to the unique circumstances found in many organizations. Their use provides irrelevant data and does not allow for proper emphasis on the particular kinds of tasks and the best ways of describing those tasks in a given organization. A better approach is to have a trained person design a tailor-made questionnaire that properly reflects the personality and unique character of the company being studied. Either this or use of a prefab questionnaire *together* with other tailored approaches such as work logs and interviews is usually required for good results.

Inadequate sampling. Gathering data in job analyses is like gathering data for any other purpose. You need enough of it to describe the entire population adequately. Sample sizes have to be large enough and data have to be gathered over a long enough period of time to assure full coverage of a work cycle. For many managerial jobs, that may mean a year or longer.

Many a data-acquisition effort has failed by insisting that people fill out questionnaires within a few days of distribution. This is not long enough for workers to contemplate the full scope of their jobs. Many companies have used work logs over a two- or three-week period, but the work cycle is two or three months. Similarly, analysts do random observations and continuous observations that do not cover a full work cycle and, therefore, are lacking in timing and sufficient quantity to give statistical confidence. Data gathering must be spread over time and provide an adequate volume of information.

Incumbents afraid of process or excessively stressed by process. Employees often do not know what the job analysis is for and do not understand it. This is cause for fear and stress. It often appears to workers that they are being watched, perhaps to find out if they are really working or to find out if perhaps someone else should be found to do the job. Incumbents often feel too that someone is trying to tinker with their jobs—someone who does not really know what the work is like and cannot possibly learn through these shaky analysis techniques. A further problem is that workers are often stressed by job analysis because they have to squeeze work logs, questionnaires, and interviews into already too hectic work schedules. Proper scheduling of job analysis efforts and, again, proper orientation of workers can avoid these problems.

Data-providing for the JD not listed as a responsibility. Few companies make either the subordinate or the supervisor accountable for generating quality data for JD preparation. It is one of those things employees are expected to do every so often—and expected to do well—but it is not a responsibility written into the JDs of employees. At the end of the year no one is ever evaluated on how well they contributed to the job analysis and job description preparation effort. Neither boss nor subordinate is held accountable for JD development and updating.

A sound management practice is to list each employee's annual responsibility for providing accurate data for JD preparation in each employee's job description. You may want to indicate for given employees that they will be expected to provide data not only for their own JDs but for the JDs of work associates. This approach pulls job analysis and JD preparation out of the closet and overtly treats it as an employee obligation. Then during performance reviews, you can legitimately evaluate and discuss the employee's contribution in this area.

Costly and time consuming. Another reason JDs contain flawed content is because very little investment was ever made in gathering data for them. Job analyses, and JD preparation properly executed, can be expensive—at least until a system for gathering data and preparing JDs is established. Job analysis usually means some down time for workers and often means someone, such as an outside professional analyst, has to be paid for conducting the job analysis and perhaps writing the job descriptions. A clear problem associated with data gathering is this cost and time involved. However, without a significant investment, JDs will likely be flawed and, consequently, become a lethal management tool—especially in the hands of the uninitiated.

Use for data not decided first. Many a data-gathering effort has been like poking in a haystack to try to find the needle. The effort is excessively lengthy, it gathers data that will not be used, it challenges workers unnecessarily. Job analysis, without first deciding what data are really needed and why, is a highly inefficient—largely wasted effort. Some novice analysts wind up asking numerous questions during interviews that generate answers that are not needed.

Management and analysts must have their direction—their reason—for the data-gathering and JD preparation effort clearly in mind and must plan and structure this effort for high yield. Considerable preliminary work must be done before data generating starts. Otherwise it is like scatter bombing. You do not know where the target is so you spray the area, hoping you will hit it. You may hit it but is it worth the cost and frustration?

Subjects cannot remember everything. Techniques, such as questionnaires, interviews, and even work logs, rely on employee memory and ability to mentally capture and communicate the full scope and depth of the job. But employees, even though they do the job—and do it well—often cannot think through and recall all they do when sitting down in an interview or when filling out a questionnaire, for example.

Frequently, tasks are performed but once a year. One is likely to forget to record or report these. Other, perhaps low-priority but still time-consuming, tasks are often disregarded in reporting by incumbents. It is necessary to allow plenty of time for incumbents to think about their jobs. Analysts must be skilled in stimulating recall with appropriate questions on questionnaires and in interviews, and must have workers report at the proper intervals with work logs.

Person spec and job characteristic data confusingly mixed with data on time usage. Job analyses too frequently do not distinguish job or task dimensions from person specifications and job characteristics. Task dimensions take up time; person specs and job characteristics do not. Job analysis is often negligent in not focusing on how workers spend their time. This is the key type of information desired for preparing job descriptions, but frequently analyses slip into excessive emphasis on specs and characteristics. It is valuable to know, for example, that the worker needs such and such skills to do the job and that the job is, perhaps, rather routine or dangerous at times, but these are specs and characteristics. Most of the 132 uses of JDs discussed in Chapter 2 require hard data on time distribution—*what* the worker does and *how long* it takes. In data gathering, time-use data should clearly be separated from other data.

Formal job analyses not done. Too many companies try to write job descriptions directly, from scratch—without really *gathering* any data—or from data acquired informally. In a recent study the author found that 85 percent of the organizations surveyed had job descriptions prepared for at least some of their employees, but only 10 percent had conducted any rigorous data gathering for JD preparation. The common approach was either to have employees directly write their own JDs or to have the boss do it for the employees. Such an approach usually produces JDs in a rather short time with little pain, but the JDs produced are generally far from valid. A well-done formal data-gathering effort tends to succeed at a much higher rate because it is planned—thought through. Possible flaws are anticipated in advance and avoided. Redundancy procedures can be built in to assure acquisition of accurate data.

Higher authority not involved. Job analyses perhaps more often than not lack the blessings, guidance, and overt support of higher management echelons. Often employees are not made aware of the high priority of the job analysis as an organizational engagement. Management fails to communicate this to them. Often, also, employees see higher management avoiding subjecting themselves to job analysis efforts. Under such conditions it is difficult for employees to take job analysis seriously—as anything but a bureaucratic tack-on simply invented to maintain bureaucratic muscle and control over employee behavior.

Crisis data acquisition. Data gathering is not infrequently commonly done in a crisis. Another common scenario is for the organization to be moving along without much thought given to the desirability of job descriptions. All of a sudden someone suggests the need for some JDs. Management then rushes around trying quickly to get some together. The process is not coordinated. The types of data really needed are not identified. In short, this crisis approach produces a third-rate JD. Management then attempts to use the developed JDs but finds after a while that the JDs are not good enough to use and finally abandons them, filing them away for the long term. At some later date someone suggests the need for JDs again and the process starts all over. Sound familiar? This is the crisis approach to JD preparation—no planned, regular, continuing effort.

Too much pirating of data. When people are asked to prepare JDs apart from any formal attempt to gather data, they often look for the path of least resistance (PLR). The PLR is often to steal from other sources. Employees (supervisors and subordinates) often dig out old JDs and essentially copy them. Sometimes they get JDs that have been prepared for other workers doing similar jobs in the company or outside or take data from standardized JDs prepared by the industry or an outside professional group. Sometimes they try to piece together JDs from various other company records and documents. All these sources can help, but help must be distinguished from substitution. When a simple look-for-what-is-already-written-down-elsewhere approach is used, you get stuck with a fictitious job description.

Lack of standardized data gathering. When the interview is used for one subject, a questionnaire is used with another subject, and, say, direct observation is used with a third, you have a problem with data gathering. The data derived will defy attempts at comparison. It will be impossible to put together three JDs that provide accurate comparison of the jobs. Similarly, when one subject is allowed thirty minutes for filling out a questionnaire and another has two weeks, you have a situation that prevents valid comparison of jobs on the basis of the data collected.

Some companies are notorious for uncoordinated data gathering across departments. Production, for example, uses one type of questionnaire; the marketing department uses another type. It even gets worse, for example, when a work log sheet with predetermined categories of activities is used in one department, and a work log that leaves activity definition completely up to the incumbent is used in another department. The only way data will truly be useful company-wide is for data to be generated systematically with standardized means across employees and across departments.

Lack of help during the process. Seldom do data providers get enough advice and guidance during the process. Quality orientation for data providers is necessary but not sufficient. Incumbents are going to need help answering questions, doing logs, and performing all the other steps in the process. Those conducting the job analysis need to be readily available to provide help upon request. Indeed, they need to intervene actively—to solict questions and comments from respondents—and to search continually for ways to ease the process along. Proper intervention during the process can motivate constructive incumbent contributions too. Workers can come to sense the great importance of the analysis and how it can be of real benefit to them and the company.

Data gathered by novices. Job analyses are too commonly conducted by novices. For some reason companies have a habit of delegating job analysis work to newcomers who lack expertise and experience in the process. Perhaps this is because it is a good way to give the new person a wealth of valuable experience fast. Perhaps it is because many people consider job analysis to be a rather routine endeavor, which involves little complexity or heavy decision making. Whatever the reason, it is usually not enough to support amateurism. JD data are so vital that only those who have developed a high skill at gathering it should gather it. It may be basic stuff but it has to be done right or the organization can literally come tumbling down.

Performance data gathered. During the job analysis one does not wish to answer how well workers are performing. This determination is left for another time—during performance evaluations and reviews. Performance data are vital but have nothing to do with data about the design of the job. Job analyses that go astray and deal with performance issues are missing the point. They will never generate the data needed for a JD. You can ask what performance criteria and what performance standards exist. This can help clarify job design. But going beyond this and attempting to evaluate incumbent performance is outside the scope of the job analysis. It should not be mixed with it.

Employees find it difficult to word what they do. Job analysis efforts are frequently hampered by employees' inability to state in words what they really do. Interviews, questionnaires, and work logs all face this problem. Many fine employees struggle when asked to state what they do and to categorize into major areas of responsibility what they do. They can do the job but cannot tell you about it. To overcome this problem takes skillful interviewing, carefully worded and structured questionnaires, and work logs, such as in Appendix M, that minimize the need for written phrases by the respondent by requiring check marks instead of written phrases.

Appendixes

APPENDIX A: Job Description

Identifying Data

Position: Field Supervisor   Department/Division: Field

Line or Staff: Line   Management Level: Second   Pay Status: Salaried

Immediate Supervisor: Director of Operations

Immediate Subordinates: Assistant Field Supervisor, Shop Foreman, 4
   Field Foremen, C & D Cold Storage Supervisor, Crew Leaders

Functional Authority: To: None   From: None

Primary Location of Work: Fields and C & D Headquarters

Date Prepared/Revised: October 6, 1988   Approved By: President

Overall Purpose of Job

The general purpose of this job is to assure that all blueberry fields
are properly prepared to provide maximum yield, in terms of both quality and quantity, and to assure that all berries are properly harvested
and distributed to storage or direct processing.

Major Functions for which have Direct Responsibility

Priority   % Time

1. Preparing fields in fall, spring and summer.   35%

   A. Supervisory duties.

      a. Assigns schedules and communicates strawing, fertilizing,
         mowing, velpar application/weed control, burning, land
         clearing, bug spraying, butt spraying, bee distribution,
         road work, trash removal, and irrigation tasks to subord-
         inates.

      b. Trains and motivates as needed.

      c. Monitors progress, quality and cost of work and adjusts as
         needed (includes doing time cards).

   B. Operative Duties.

      a. Drives tractors and operates other equipment used.

      b. Services and repairs equipment in the field.

APPENDIX A (*continued*)

    c. Transports workers and equipment to and from fields.

    d. Helps put out bees.

2. Monitoring, repairing and building farm equipment.   17%

   A. Supervisory duties.

      a. Plans what field and transportation equipment to repair, build and perform preventive maintenance on.

      b. Schedules, assigns and communicates maintenance, repair and building tasks to Shop Foreman.

      c. Trains and motivates as needed.

      d. Monitors progress, quality and cost of work and makes needed adjustments (includes doing time cards).

   B. Operative duties.

      a. Fixes and services equipment.

      b. Works on building new equipment.

      c. Tests repaired equipment.

3. Harvesting fields during blueberry season.   9%

   A. Supervisory duties.

      a. Hires crew leaders and assigns to fields.

      b. Provides orientation for crew leaders.

      c. Schedules picking.

      d. Trains and motivates as needed.

      e. Monitors progress, quality and cost of work and adjusts as needed (includes checking how "clean" the picking is done).

   B. Operative duties.

   (Minimal)

APPENDIX A (*continued*)

4. Receiving and shipping fresh berries at C & D.   9%

    A. Supervisory duties.

        a. Assigns and communicates unloading, and storage tasks, relative to fresh berries arriving from the field, to subordinates.

        b. Assigns and communicates fresh berry loading tasks to workers.

        c. Monitors progress, quality and cost of work and adjusts as needed (includes doing time cards).

    B. Operative duties.

        a. Unloads trucks arriving from the field.

        b. Loads trucks for shipment of berries to outside storage.

        c. Moves unloaded berries into proper storage location.

5. Preparing and closing housing for rakers.   9%

    A. Supervisory duties.

        a. Schedules, assigns and communicates camp clean up, electricity hook up/shut off, water hook up/shut off, sewage systems readying, camp moving, camp rebuilding, camp repairing, camp cleaning and rodent control tasks to subordinates.

        b. Trains and motivates as needed.

        c. Monitors progress, quality and cost of work and adjusts as needed (includes doing time cards).

    B. Operative duties.

    Performs all housing preparation and closing tasks.

% Time

6. Purchasing parts, equipment, tools and bees.   4%

   A. Supervisory duties.

      a. Determines what to order from whom and when, and assigns many of the ordering tasks to the Cold Storage Supervisor.

      b. Assigns and schedules workers to transport, receive and/or store items ordered.

      c. Trains and motivates as needed.

      d. Monitors arrival time on orders and quality of merchandise ordered, and adjusts as needed.

   B. Operative duties.

      a. Places some orders.

      b. Receives orders and properly stores.

      c. Drives truck to pick up some orders.

7. Operating the C & D freezer.   4%

   A. Supervisory duties.

      a. Assigns and communicates responsibilities to the Cold Storage Supervisor at C & D.

      b. Assigns and schedules help for the Cold Storage Supervisor.

      c. Trains and motivates as needed.

      d. Monitors progress, quality and cost of work and adjusts as needed.

   B. Operative duties.

   (Minimal)

	% Time
8. Engaging in <u>other</u> activities.	13%

A. Routine: Prepares reports. Deals with employee personal matters, accidents and illnesses. Safeguards equipment. Clears work area. Helps with snow removal. Meets with salespeople. Handles chemical inventory.

B. Temporary (this <u>coming</u> year):

C. Group work: Attends management meetings.

D. Unplanned work (this <u>past</u> year): Responded to unexpected plant disease. Serviced unexpected breakdowns of equipment. Met with fire and blueberry inspectors. Dealt with outside grower problems. Responded to natural disasters.

E. Non/semi-work: Travels. Takes breaks. Socializes. Waits out delays.

Asset Accountability

	$ Value
1. Equipment--irrigation pipes and pumps, trucks, tractors, machinery, etc.	$ 636,000
2. Buildings at C & D, camps and showroom	2,325,000
3. Land (berry and wood)	$16,800,000

Working Conditions

1. Hazards: Moving equipment. Sprays. Natural hazards such as washouts, hills, rocks. Frozen ground. Fumes from chemical sprayers, tractors and burners.

2. Physical environment: Hot at times. Noise from equipment. Dirty shop environment and dust in field. Fumes from freezer compressor. Pleasant in office. Clean air, generally, in fields.

3. Stress/emotional demands: Some stress to get seasonal jobs done when weather not accommodating.

4. Social environment: Always people to talk and work with.

5. Mental and physical demands: Often there is much work to do in a short time due to changing weather conditions.

Appendix A is by courtesy of Jasper Wyman and Son Co., Milbridge, Maine

APPENDIX B: Person Specification

This person specification is for a warehouse supervisor in a canning company. A more fully developed and more useful person spec might identify the relative importance of each dimension, clearly define the required level or degree of each dimension, and provide scales for rating employees or candidates on each dimension. Also, these person specs are more useful if they show the association between specific tasks in the JD and specs. That is, each different task/responsibility can be listed and indicated with each task/responsibility the required skills, abilities, knowledge, and qualifications can be listed.

1. Considerable experience in all phases of warehouse operation, maintenance, shipping and receiving.

2. Formal training in statistical acceptance sampling techniques.

3. Human relations and verbal communication skills.

4. Skill in driving forklifts and trucks.

5. Ability to work with numbers.

6. Some knowledge of standard accounting practices.

7. Knowledge of inventory control principles and methods.

8. Organizing skills.

9. Physical muscle.

10. Ability to adapt to rapidly changing assignments and to conflicting job assignments.

11. Knowledge of packaging materials--strengths and weaknesses of various materials for protecting goods.

12. Understanding of the purchasing function in business.

13. Desire to keep work surroundings neat and clean.

14. Six months' experience in using the computer for inventory control and quality control.

APPENDIX C: Procedure and Method

Both procedures and methods spell out a sequence of steps to take to accomplish something. A method is more detailed than a procedure. A procedure may involve several people, oral or written instructions, information, as well as materials, etc., to be exchanged, forms to be filled out, checkings and verifications to be made. The recurring activity governed by a procedure is not just a repetitive task at a work station--not, for instance, typing a letter or filing one. What the typist and the file clerk are doing is termed an operation. Such an operation would be a step in a procedure. The equipment used and the motions involved in performing an operation--the way the operation is performed--is the <u>method</u>. Methods spell out detailed required movements.

Example of a procedure (for contract shipments)

Step   Description

1. At the earliest date on which the Project Engineer can reasonably anticipate when equipment will be shipped on his/her project, he/she should notify all people concerned with the shipment of the schedule. Two weeks' advance notice is desirable and preferably will be given with an internal memorandum. Schedule delay or acceleration deserves the same notifications.

    A tickler file will be maintained by Contracts Administration to provide an advance check for all projects in the laboratory.

2. The Project Engineer will request of Technical Liaison information regarding the destination of the equipment, the type of packing required (domestic or overseas) and the level of classification.

3. Technical Liaison will inquire of USASERU to obtain the desired information and will transmit it back to the Project Engineer.

4. The Project Engineer will advise the Packing group of his/her requirements. He/she will provide the following information:

    a. Itemized list of all units to be shipped, <u>including</u> quantities, full description and serial numbers.

    b. Type of packing (will some packing boxes also be used as permanent cases?)

APPENDIX C (*continued*)

<u>Step</u>   <u>Description</u>

    c.   Security classification.

    d.   Spare parts list.

Example of a method (for stocking lumber at a point of use)

1.   Pick up 1 piece 4" x 4" x 8'.

2.   Carry to truck.

3.   Pile on truck.

4.   Move to 23" mill by truck.

5.   Pick up 1 piece 4" x 4" x 8'.

6.   Move to storage pile by hand.

7.   Place on pile.

8.   Hold for usage.

9.   Pick up 1 piece 4" x 4" x 8'.

10. Carry to car.

11. Place in car.

Source: Adapted from William M. Berliner and William J. McLarney, *Management Practice and Training* (Homewood, Ill.: Richard D. Irwin, 1974), pp. 171 and 289. The example of a procedure is by courtesy of Sylvania Electric Products, Electronic Defense Laboratory, Mountain View, California. The example of a method is from the Methods Engineering Manual, 1951, by courtesy of the U.S. Steel Company.

APPENDIX D: Performance Evaluation Instrument

The following is part of a sample performance assessment instrument for measuring the performance of a secretary. Each scale represents a performance criterion. The designated acceptable ranges are performance standards.

Importance
(1-10)

1. Quality of letter typing.   3

```
                              |------Acceptable Range------|
|_____|_____|_____|_____|
1              2              3              4              5
Very Poor      Poor           Average        Good     Very Good
```

Very poor=4+ errors per letter.
Average=1 error per letter.
Very good=0 errors per 10 letters.

2. Timeliness of getting work done.   8

```
                                          |--Acceptable-|
                                          |----Range----|
|_____|_____|_____|_____|
1              2              3              4              5
Very Poor      Poor           Average        Good     Very Good
```

Very poor=Has work done on time less than 50% of time.
Average=Has work done on time 75% of time.
Very good=Has work done on time 100% of time.

3. Materials waste (a cost).   5

```
                                          |--Acceptable-|
                                          |----Range----|
|_____|_____|_____|_____|
1              2              3              4              5
Very Poor      Poor           Average        Good     Very Good
```

Very poor=10% or more waste.
Average=5% waste.
Very good=3% or less waste.

APPENDIX D (*continued*)

4. Quality of guest greetings.   3

```
                             |------Acceptable Range------|
|_____|_____|_____|_____|
1              2              3              4              5
Very Poor      Poor        Average         Good       Very Good
```

Very poor=Pleasant less than 50% of time. Only gives out
  information requested. Never volunteers information.
Average=Pleasant 75% of time. Gives wrong information 20%
  of time or does not volunteer needed information.
Very good=Always pleasant. Always gives proper information
  requested by visitors. Always volunteers needed information not requested.

5. Cleanliness and neatness of office.   9

```
                                              |Accept+
                                              | able |
                                              | Range|
|_____|_____|_____|_____|
1              2              3              4        5
Very Poor      Poor        Average         Good   Very Good
```

Very poor=Never clean and always cluttered.
Average=Generally clean but cluttered 50% of the time.
Very good=Always spotless and neat.

APPENDIX E: Rules, Regulations, and Policies

Rules spell out precisely what behavior is expected of a person. They are formulated by the organization. A regulation spells out behavior required by law or by agencies charged with administering the law. Policies are guideline statements developed by the organization. They indicate, in a general way, what behavior should be like, but allow for discretion in decision making. Following are examples of each of these kinds of plans.

Sample Rules

1. No smoking is allowed in the cafeteria.

2. Employees who are absent more than 5 days per month for twelve months in succession without a medical excuse, will be dismissed.

3. All letters to VIPs must be typed on the highest quality white bond paper.

Sample Regulations

1. Employers must pay wages at or above the Federal and State minimums.

2. All visitors to the plant must wear hard hats or other protective head gear when touring the plant.

3. The company cannot dump raw sewage into the river.

Sample Policy Statements

1. It is this company's policy to let all store-level department managers resolve customer complaints.

2. One of this organization's policies is to promote from within.

3. This company's policy is to always be in the public eye.

APPENDIX F: Objectives

Objectives are statements of targets or desired accomplishments. They rather precisely define what is to be achieved and when. They often relate to upgrading or improvement efforts or to new task--new venture--pursuits. Here are some examples:

1. To produce 1,000,000 tons of fiber by 6:00 p.m. on the 30th of next month.

2. To obtain a master's degree in business within 3 years.

3. To get 80% of our customers to do repeat business with us.

4. To learn key boarding skills by March 11 of this year.

5. To increase profits by 5% in the third quarter.

6. To reduce insect infestation in our crops by 15% this year.

7. To read three books during the next month.

8. To install new furniture at a cost of less than $3,000 sometime this year.

9. To increase production by 12% during the coming quarter.

10. To reduce the number of defective items by 2% by the 14th of July.

APPENDIX G: Job Design Quality Factors

The following are aspects of job design that can be <u>evaluated</u> for appropriateness by study of the job description.

1. Discreteness of tasks versus task integration.

2. Degree of confinement to given physical position.

3. Quality of social work environment.

4. Quality of physical work environment.

5. Job scope (task variety).

6. Job depth (amount of self-planning and control built into job)

7. Task uncertainty.

8. Degree of supervisory responsibility.

9. Degree of temporary work.

10. Degree of committee or group work.

11. Appropriateness of time of work.

12. Adequacy of sources of performance feedback to worker.

13. Adequacy of sources of resource input.

14. Appropriateness of output destinations.

15. Efficiency of work layout.

16. Quality of machinery/tools used.

17. Task time distribution.

18. Task priorities.

19. Task identity.

20. Task significance.

21. Access to advice or help.

22. Utility of administrative relations.

23. Task frequency.

24. Task seasonality.

25. Task specificity.

26. Percentage of time idle.

27. Percentage of time spent on non-work/semi-work.

28. Adequacy of amount of independent authority.

29. Task complexity.

30. Rapidity of task set change.

31. Stability of task patterns.

32. Degree of task serialization.

33. Work load.

APPENDIX H: Job Analysis Questionnaire

This questionnaire is designed to provide information about your job. This information will be highly valuable for the company. It will be used for a variety of purposes chief among which are these:

1. To help in preparing accurate and comprehensive job descriptions.

2. To help in developing a more equitable and more motivational pay system.

3. To help in determining training requirements.

4. To help in upgrading the design of the work you do.

5. To help in employee recruitment, selection, and promotion.

6. To help in designing an objective system of employee performance evaluation.

Look over the entire questionnaire to get an overview of what you are being asked. Then take your time answering the questions. Think about them over two or three weeks. Jot down answers to questions, on scrap paper, as they occur to you. Fill out one of these as a rough draft first if you wish. At the end of three weeks try to completely "fill in" a final copy of this form. Use attachments where additional space is needed.

The need for forthrightness, truthfulness, accuracy, clarity, comprehensiveness and detail must be emphasized. This will not be easy. It will take a considerable amount of time. You may well become frustrated and disenchanted with this exercise. All that is asked is that you give it your best shot. Going through this exercise should enlighten you about your job!

Data from this survey will be combined with data obtained by other means from other sources. Data from all means and sources will be carefully reviewed, inconsistencies and deficiencies identified and follow-up action taken "to correct the flaws." Please bear with the process. Management is fully supportive of this effort in the interest of benefiting you and the company.

Any official documents prepared from this data will be reviewed with you and your supervisor to assure accuracy and acceptability.

In the first part of this survey we want to find out how you spend your time at work--how you divide your time among various kinds of duties and activities. Use a pencil because you may want to change check marks, words and/or time percentages as you go through this and as you begin to think more in-depth about your job. When the time percentage totals for sections A, B, C, D, E, F, and G are added, they should equal 100%. You may wish to start with section B.

PART I. A--*Regular Supervisory Work*   **% of time**
                                                                    TOTAL _____

Please check the following supervisory-type activities you regularly engage in and indicate the approximate percentage of time over the course of a year that you spend on each.

A. Planning   **% of time**
                                                       SUB-TOTAL _____

    ____1. Deciding what work needs to be done in your area, as well as where, when, how, by whom and with what.   _____

    ____2. Developing budgets.   _____

    ____3. Supplying resources for people to get work done.   _____

    ____4. Other (please specify)_____   _____

B. Communicating   **% of time**
                                                       SUB-TOTAL _____

    ____1. Assigning work to people, giving instructions, issuing directives.   _____

    ____2. Receiving instructions and directives from superiors.   _____

    ____3. Coordinating with peers.   _____

    ____4. Reporting to your superior on progress, problems, opportunities, etc.   _____

    ____5. Giving advice and recommendations.   _____

    ____6. Listening to issues and problems from subordinates.   _____

    ____7. Other (please specify)_____   _____

C. Solving problems   **% of time**
                                                       SUB-TOTAL _____

    ____1. Production/work related problems.   _____

    ____2. Equipment/tool/facility problems.   _____

    ____3. Materials/resource problems.   _____

    ____4. Personnel problems involving counseling, grievances, gripes, personal issues, etc.   _____

    ____5. Finding better ways to do things.   _____

    ____6. Other (please specify)_____   _____

D. Hiring   **% of time**
                                                       SUB-TOTAL _____

    ____1. Interviewing candidates.   _____

    ____2. Orienting new people.   _____

    ____3. Other (please specify)_____   _____

APPENDIX H (*continued*)

E. Training and development   **% of time**
                                                    SUB-TOTAL _____

    ____1. Coaching employees on how to do their jobs.   _____

    ____2. Helping employees boost performance to a higher
           level.   _____

    ____3. Other (please specify)_____   _____

F. Motivating, influencing and satisfying employees   **% of time**
                                                    SUB-TOTAL _____

    ____1. Recognizing and rewarding your subordinates,
           building morale.   _____

    ____2. Influencing or persuading your peers.   _____

    ____3. Influencing or persuading your superior.   _____

    ____4. Other (please specify)_____   _____

G. Controlling performance   **% of time**
                                                    SUB-TOTAL _____

    ____1. Inspecting, testing quality.   _____

    ____2. Checking on progress, keeping work on track.   _____

    ____3. Taking corrective action to resolve detected
           performance problems.   _____

    ____4. Disciplining and terminating.   _____

    ____5. Measuring performance.   _____

    ____6. Checking on costs.   _____

    ____7. Other (please specify)_____   _____

H. Other areas (such as preparing reports, safeguarding   % of time
equipment, dealing with accidents or illnesses, hand-   SUB-
ling personnel matters such as overtime, time off,   TOTAL _____
job changes, etc.)

    ____1._____   _____

    ____2._____   _____

    ____3._____   _____

    ____4._____   _____

Notes of importance for PART I. A._____

_____

_____

APPENDIX H (*continued*)

PART I. B--*Regular Non-Supervisory (Operative) Work*   **% of time**
                                                                  TOTAL _____

Please provide an itemized and prioritized list of regular specific duties
and responsibilities you have that are non-supervisory in nature. Start
each duty statement with an action verb such as drive, stack, spread,
clean, fix, operate, etc. Indicate, if possible, in each statement approximately how often the work is done, what tools and equipment are used, who
else might be involved and where it is done. Try also to indicate what the
outcome or result of the activity is. Indicate the approximate percentage
of time over the course of a year that you spend on each duty. Use attachments if more space is needed.

A. Daily duties and responsibilities   **% of time**
                                                                  SUB-TOTAL _____

1._____   _____

2._____   _____

3._____   _____

4._____   _____

5._____   _____

6._____   _____

7._____   _____

8._____   _____

9._____   _____

10._____   _____

11._____   _____

12._____   _____

13._____   _____

14._____   _____

15._____   _____

16._____   _____

17._____   _____

18._____   _____

19._____   _____

20._____   _____

Notes of importance:_____

_____

_____

APPENDIX H (*continued*)

B. **Weekly duties and responsibilities**   **% of time**
                                                                    SUB-TOTAL _____

1. _____   _____
2. _____   _____
3. _____   _____
4. _____   _____
5. _____   _____
6. _____   _____
7. _____   _____
8. _____   _____
9. _____   _____
10. _____   _____
11. _____   _____
12. _____   _____
13. _____   _____
14. _____   _____
15. _____   _____

Notes of importance:_____

_____

C. **Monthly or seasonal duties and responsibilities**   **% of time**
                                                                  SUB-TOTAL _____

1. _____   _____
2. _____   _____
3. _____   _____
4. _____   _____
5. _____   _____
6. _____   _____
7. _____   _____
8. _____   _____
9. _____   _____
10. _____   _____
11. _____   _____
12. _____   _____
13. _____   _____
14. _____   _____
15. _____   _____

Notes of importance:_____

_____

APPENDIX H (*continued*)

PART I

D. Annual duties and responsibilities   % of time

SUB-TOTAL _____

1. _____ _____
2. _____ _____
3. _____ _____
4. _____ _____
5. _____ _____
6. _____ _____
7. _____ _____
8. _____ _____
9. _____ _____
10. _____ _____
11. _____ _____
12. _____ _____
13. _____ _____
14. _____ _____
15. _____ _____

Notes of importance:_____

_____

PART I. *C--Temporary Assignments (Planned in Advance) for
this past year*   % of time

TOTAL _____

A. _____ _____
B. _____ _____
C. _____ _____
D. _____ _____
E. _____ _____
F. _____ _____

Notes of importance:_____

_____

PART I. *D--Committee, Group or Task Force Involvement
for this past year*   % of time

TOTAL _____

A. _____ _____
B. _____ _____
C. _____ _____
D. _____ _____
E. _____ _____
F. _____ _____

Notes of importance:_____

_____

APPENDIX H (*continued*)

PART I

PART I. **E--Processing Unusual Directives, requests, self-initiatives, and/or problems this past year (spur-of-the-moment)**   TOTAL _____   **% of time**

A._____   _____

B._____   _____

C._____   _____

D._____   _____

E._____   _____

F._____   _____

G._____   _____

H._____   _____

Notes of importance:_____

PART I. **F--Average Non-Work or Semi-Work Time (please check any that apply during the course of a year)**   TOTAL _____   **% of time**

____A. Travel time.   _____

____B. Break/rest time.   _____

____C. On-the-job socializing.   _____

____D. Delay time (waiting for other things to happen).   _____

____E. Other (please specify)_____   _____

Notes of importance:_____

PART I. **G--If there is anything you spend time on that does not seem to fit above, describe it here and indicate the approximate percentage of time, during the course of a year, spent on it.**   TOTAL _____   **% of time**

_____

_____

_____

_____

NOTE: Please indicate here any of the above duties that you generally <u>share</u> with someone else. State <u>who</u> else.

131

APPENDIX H (*continued*)

<u>*P A R T   II*</u>

In the second part of this survey we want to find out a number of other things about your job besides how you spend your time.

PART II.   A--Major Accountabilities

Please indicate here the key "things" you are supposed to make sure get done, and get done right, in this company. These are the major results or outcomes for which management should hold you responsible.

A._____

B._____

C._____

D._____

E._____

F._____

G._____

H._____

PART II.   B--Independent Authority

Please indicate here the extent of authority you have to make decisions committing the organization's resources. Which decisions can you make and which must you clear with higher authority?

A. **Can you make equipment purchase decisions?**

    Yes _____   No _____   Some _____

    Explain_____

    _____

B. **Can you "get rid" of old equipment as you see fit?**

    Yes _____   No _____   Some _____

    Explain_____

    _____

C. **Can you hire and fire personnel? Make disciplinary decisions?**

    Yes _____   No _____   Some _____

    Explain_____

    _____

D. **Can you spend company dollars as long as you are within your budget?**

    Yes _____   No _____   Some _____

    Explain_____

    _____

E. **What major changes can you make in your area without higher authority's ok?**

    List and explain_____

    _____

    _____

    _____

    _____

APPENDIX H (*continued*)

PART II

F. Other key areas in which you can or cannot make your own decisions?

Please explain_____

_____

_____

_____

PART II. C--Responsibility for Company Assets

Please indicate below what equipment, tools, facilities, inventories, land and other resources or assets you are charged with protecting and using properly.

approximate
$ value

A._____ _____

B._____ _____

C._____ _____

D._____ _____

E._____ _____

F._____ _____

G._____ _____

H._____ _____

I._____ _____

J._____ _____

K._____ _____

L._____ _____

M._____ _____

PART II. D--Relations with Other Employees

A. Who is your immediate supervisor?_____

B. From whom besides your immediate supervisor do you take orders/ directives?_____

C. How many regular, full-time subordinates do you have?_____

D. Briefly describe the work of each of your regular subordinates:

_____

_____

_____

_____

_____

_____

_____

_____

_____

_____

PART II

D. (continued)

_____

_____

_____

_____

_____

_____

_____

_____

_____

E. With whom, besides your boss and subordinates do you "work" most frequently? <u>Doing what?</u>

_____

_____

_____

_____

Part II. E--Working Conditions

Please give a short description for each item below.

A. Any hazards on your job?_____

_____

_____

_____

B. Nature of the physical work environment--heat, light, noise, fumes,
dirt, etc._____

_____

_____

_____

C. Any stresses or emotional demands?_____

_____

_____

_____

D. The social environment: Are there people to talk to? Do you work alone?
Do you meet new people all the time?_____

_____

_____

E. Mental and physical demands on your job?_____

_____

_____

_____

APPENDIX H (*continued*)

PART II

PART II. F--Tools and Equipment You Need to Know How to Use

Please list any tools or equipment you must know how to use or operate on your job.

A._____

B._____

C._____

D._____

E._____

F._____

G._____

H._____

I._____

J._____

PART II. G--Education or Training Requirements for Your Job

Please indicate how much education and what type of education are minimal requirements for this job. Indicate any special formal training required for this job.

	Kind of education or training	How much?
A.	_____	_____
B.	_____	_____
C.	_____	_____
D.	_____	_____
E.	_____	_____
F.	_____	_____
G.	_____	_____
H.	_____	_____
I.	_____	_____

PART II. H--Experience Needed

Please indicate how much experience and what kind of experience one should have to do this job well.

	Kind of experience	How much?
A.	_____	_____
B.	_____	_____
C.	_____	_____
D.	_____	_____
E.	_____	_____
F.	_____	_____
G.	_____	_____
H.	_____	_____
I.	_____	_____
J.	_____	_____

APPENDIX H (*continued*)

PART II

PART II. I--Skills, Abilities and Knowledge

Please list as many specific kinds of skills and types of knowledge you should have to do this job. For example, do you need typing skill, computer knowledge, human relations skills, physical muscle, good hand-eye coordination and quickness? Is acute eyesight important? Do you need knowledge of accounting practices and mechanics? Do you need knowledge of chemicals? Do you need skill at driving vehicles? Do you need ability to deal with numbers? Etc. Please list in order of importance (the most important first).

Kind of specific skills, abilities and knowledge required

A._____

B._____

C._____

D._____

E._____

F._____

G._____

H._____

I._____

J._____

K._____

Part II. J--General Job Identification Data

A. **Where** do you spend most of your time while on this job?_____

B. **Where** can you be found the second most often?_____

C. Is your job exempt or non-exempt?_____

D. What is the title of your job?_____

E. What department or division of the company is your job in?_____

_____

PART II. K--Job Purpose

Please briefly explain the general purpose of your job. Sum it all up. Why does your job exist? Write a brief statement of your function or role in the organization._____

_____

_____

PART II. L--How Your Job Should be Changed in Content

A. Please list any "things" you now are expected to do, but don't really think you should be doing or should have to do._____

_____

B. Please list any "things" you now do not do, but think you really should.

_____

_____

PART II. M--Signature and Date

A. Signature_____ B. Date_____

APPENDIX I: Managerial Positions Description Questionnaire (MPDQ)

Below is a section of the MPDQ.

To achieve organizational goals, managers and consultants may be required to communicate with employees at many levels within the corporation and with influential people outside the corporation. The purposes of these contacts may include such functions as:

- Informing
- Receiving information
- Influencing
- Promoting
- Selling

- Directing
- Coordinating
- Integrating
- Negotiating

Directions:

Describe the nature of your contacts by completing the chart as follows:

Step 1: Mark an "X" in the box to the left of the kinds of individuals that represent your major contacts internal and external to Control Data Corporation.

Step 2: For each contact checked, print a number between 0 and 4 in each column to indicate how significant a part of your position that PURPOSE is. (Remember to consider both its *importance* in light of all other position activities and its *frequency* of occurrence.)

0 – Definitely not part of the position.
1 – A minor part of the position.
2 – A moderate part of the position.
3 – A substantial part of the position.
4 – A crucial and most significant part of the position.

Step 3: If you have any other contacts please elaborate on their nature and purpose below:

_____

_____

_____

_____

Source: Adapted from John M. Ivancevich and William F. Gluech, *Foundations of Personnel* (Plano, Tex.: Business Publications, 1983), pp. 118–19. The section of the MPDQ is by courtesy of the Control Data Corporation.

SECTION OF THE MPDQ

CONTACTS	**PURPOSE**				
INTERNAL	Share information regarding past, present or anticipated activities or decisions	Influence others to act or decide in a manner consistent with my objectives	Direct and/or integrate the plans, activities, or decisions of others		
Executive or senior vice president and above	159	167	175	183	
Vice president	160	168	176	184	
General/regional manager, director, or executive consultant	161	169	177	185	
Department/district manager, or senior consultant	162	170	178	186	
Section/branch manager or consultant	163	171	179	187	
Unit manager	164	172	180	188	
Exempt employees	165	173	181	189	
Nonexempt employees	166	174	182	190	
EXTERNAL	Provide, obtain or exchange information or advice	Promote the organization or its products/services	Influence others to act or decide in a manner consistent with my objectives	Sell products/services	Negotiate contracts, settlements, etc.
Customers at a level equivalent to or above a Control Data general/regional manager	191	198	205	212	219
Customers at a level lower than a Control Data general/regional manager	192	199	206	213	220
Representatives of major suppliers, for example, joint ventures, subcontractors for major contracts	193	200	207	214	221
Employees of suppliers who provide Control Data with parts or services	194	201	208	215	222
Representatives of influential community organizations	195	202	209	216	223
Individuals such as applicants, stockholders	196	203	210	217	224
Representatives of federal or state governments such as defense contract auditors, government inspectors, etc.	197	204	211	218	225

APPENDIX J: Position Analysis Questionnaire (PAQ)

Below is a portion of a completed page from the Position Analysis Questionnaire.

INFORMATION INPUT

1. INFORMATION INPUT

    1.1 Sources of Job Information

    Rate each of the following items in terms of the extent to which it
    is used by the worker as a source of information in performing his
    job.

    Extent of Use (U)

    NA Does not apply
     1 Nominal/very infrequent
     2 Occasional
     3 Moderate
     4 Considerable
     5 Very substantial

    1.1.1 Visual Sources of Job Information

1|4 Written materials (books, reports, office notes, articles, job
     instructions, signs, etc.)

2|2 Quantitative materials (materials which deal with quantities or
     amounts, such as graphs, accounts, specifications, tables of
     numbers, etc.)

3|1 Pictorial materials (pictures or picturelike materials used as
     sources of information, for example, drawings, blueprints, diagrams,
     maps, tracings, photographic films, x-ray films, TV pictures, etc.)

4|1 Patterns/related devices (templates, stencils, patterns, etc., used
     as *sources* of information when *observed* during use; do *not* include
     here materials described in item 3 above)

5|2 Visual displays (dials, gauges, signal lights, radarscopes, speed-
     meters, clocks, etc.)

6|5   Measuring devices (rulers, calipers, tire pressure gauges, scales, thickness gauges, pipettes, thermometers, protractors, etc., used to obtain visual information about physical measurements; do *not* include here devices described in item 5 above)

7|4   Mechanical devices (tools, equipment, machinery, and other mechanical devices which are *sources* of information when *observed* during use or operation)

8|3   Materials in process (parts, materials, objects, etc., which are *sources* of information when being modified, worked on, or otherwise processed, such as bread dough being mixed, workpiece being turned in a lathe, fabric being cut, shoe being resoled, etc.)

9|4   Materials *not* in process (parts, materials, objects, etc., not in the process of being changed or modified, which are *sources* of information when being inspected, handled, packaged, distributed, or selected, etc., such as items or materials in inventory, storage, or distribution channels, items being inspected, etc.)

10|3   Features of nature (landscapes, fields, geological samples, vegetation, cloud formations, and other features of nature which are observed or inspected to provide information)

11|2   Man-made features of environment (structures, buildings, dams, highways, bridges, docks, railroads, and other "man-made" or altered aspects of the indoor or outdoor environment which are *observed* or *inspected* to provide job information; do not consider equipment, machines, etc., that an individual uses in his work, as covered by item 7)

Source: Adapted from Michael R. Carrell and Frank E. Kuzmits, *Personnel* (Columbus, Ohio: Charles E. Merrill, 1982), p. 79. The section of the PAQ is by courtesy of the Occupational Research Center, Department of Psychological Sciences, Purdue University, West Lafayette, Indiana.

APPENDIX K: Quantitative Task Inventory (QTI)

Below is a section from a tailor-made quantitative task inventory.

TASKS Be sure to use a No.2 pencil only and blacken out appropriate letters and numbers completely.	A Task NOT performed-- zero time spent and zero importance	B Indicate relative time spent			C Indicate relative importance			D Task is typically performed		
		Much less than other tasks	About the same as other tasks	Much more than other tasks	Much less than other tasks	About the same as other tasks	Much more than other tasks	On site in plant	Both plants equally	In control room
F. Operating turbogenerators										
1. Prepare turbine for start-up following established procedures.	N	1	2	3	4	5	1 2 3 4 5	1	2	3
2. Inspect, monitor, and/or operate turning gear drive and emergency backup systems.	N	1	2	3	4	5	1 2 3 4 5	1	2	3
3. Monitor and operate turbine bypass or condenser steam dump system.	N	1	2	3	4	5	1 2 3 4 5	1	2	3
4. Bring turbine up to speed following established procedures.	N	1	2	3	4	5	1 2 3 4 5	1	2	3
5. Monitor and control turbine temperature differentials.	N	1	2	3	4	5	1 2 3 4 5	1	2	3

TASKS Be sure to use a No. 2 pencil only and blacken out appropriate letters and numbers completely.	A Task NOT performed-- zero time spent and zero importance	B Much less than other tasks	About the same as other tasks	Much more than other tasks	C Much less than other tasks	About the same as other tasks	Much more than other tasks	D On site in plant	Both plants equally	In control room
M. Operating nuclear reactors										
1. Know and follow NRC regulatory requirements (license and tech specs).	N	1	2 3	4 5	1	2 3	4 5	1	2	3
2. Maintain security of controlled copies of operating procedures to ensure that current copy is always present in control room.	N	1	2 3	4 5	1	2 3	4 5	1	2	3
3. Perform plant heat balance to calibrate nuclear instrumentation.	N	1	2 3	4 5	1	2 3	4 5	1	2	3
4. Start up reactor.	N	1	2 3	4 5	1	2 3	4 5	1	2	3
5. Monitor reactor core parameters and log readings from control room instrumentation.	N	1	2 3	4 5	1	2 3	4 5	1	2	3
6. Manipulate reactor controls to adjust reactivity for load changes.	N	1	2 3	4 5	1	2 3	4 5	1	2	3
7. Coordinate and perform surveillance tests as prescribed by tech specs.	N	1	2 3	4 5	1	2 3	4 5	1	2	3
8. Monitor and operate reactor coolant system.	N	1	2 3	4 5	1	2 3	4 5	1	2	3
9. Monitor and operate component cooling systems.	N	1	2 3	4 5	1	2 3	4 5	1	2	3

Source: Adapted from George T. Milkovich and Jerry M. Newman, *Compensation* (Plano, Tex.: Business Publications, 1984), p. 64. The section of the QTI is from the Plant Operator Work Behavior List by courtesy of the Personnel Decision Research Institute for the Edison Electric Institute.

APPENDIX L: Work (Time) Log for Non-Managers

Time	Description of tasks (what I did)	Time Spent	Unit Vol.	Location (where I did it)	Others Involved			
					Name	Location	Mode of contract	Length of contract
7-8	1 2 3 4 5 6							
8-9	1 2 3 4 5 6							
9-10	1 2 3 4 5 6							
10-11	1 2 3 4 5 6							
11-12	1 2 3 4 5 6							
12-1	1 2 3 4 5 6							
1-2	1 2 3 4 5 6							
2-3	1 2 3 4 5 6							

APPENDIX M: Time Log for Managers

TIME	Planning & preparing	Giving instructions, advice & assignments	In meeting--consultation	Paperwork	On phone	Motivating and/or training	Checking progress, quality, cost	Reading or self-development	Solving problems	Receiving advice, instructions, assignments	Operative (non-supervisory work)	Non-work, semi-work	Other	Description
8 - 8:30														
8:30 - 9														
9 - 9:30														
9:30 - 10														
10 - 10:30														
10:30 - 11														
11 - 11:30														
11:30 - 12														
FILL IN														
12 - 12:30														
12:30 - 1														
1 - 1:30														
1:30 - 2														
2 - 2:30														
2:30 - 3														
3 - 3:30														
3:30 - 4														
4 - 4:30														
4:30 - 5														
FILL IN														
OTHER														

Name _____
Position _____
Dept. _____
Date _____

NOTES

APPENDIX N: Random Observation Sheet

Do four random observations per day per person for four weeks.

Person Observed: _____

	Monday		Tuesday		Wednesday		Thursday		Friday	
	Time	What Observed	Time	What Observed	Time	What Observed	Time	What Observed	Time	What Observed
Week #1										
Week #2										
Week #3										
Week #4										

145

APPENDIX O: Job Factor Sheet

Job factor sheets contain criteria (factors) for <u>evaluating</u> jobs and "anchored" scales (sometimes called degrees) for measuring the degree to which factors are required on particular jobs. An anchored scale is a scale which contains descriptions of what each point along the scale represents. Such descriptions allow for more objective assessment. The criteria in a job factor sheet may involve dimensions about the job such as amount of resources the incumbent controls, job hazards, etc., <u>and</u> dimensions related to person specifications such as education or skill requirements. Following is a sample job factor sheet.

<u>FACTOR A - SKILLS</u>

<u>Degree</u>	<u>Education</u>	<u>Points</u>*
1	Ability to read and write only	5
2	High school graduate or equivalent	10
3	Some college	15
4	College degree or equivalent	20

<u>Degree</u>	<u>Experience and Training</u>	<u>Points</u>
1	Less than 1 week	10
2	1 week to 1 month	20
3	1 to 6 months	30
4	More than 6 months	40

<u>Degree</u>	<u>Initiative</u>	<u>Points</u>
1	Receives constant instruction from supervisor	5
2	Frequent attention and instruction from supervisor	10
3	Infrequent supervision; must make decisions	15
4	Works most of the time on his own	20

APPENDIX O (*continued*)

FACTOR B - RESPONSIBILITY

Degree	Equipment	Points
1	No responsibility for equipment	20
2	Limited responsibility - supervision frequent	20
3	Damages could occur	30
4	Errors could cause considerable damage	40

Degree	Materials	Points
1	Handles valuable materials only under supervision	15
2	Infrequent materials handling on own - usually supervised	30
3	Worker must exercise care - some handling individually	45
4	Frequently handles valuable materials - responsible for safety	60

Degree	Work of Others	Points
1	No responsibility for others	10
2	Some supervision of others	20
3	Supervises work of from 1 to 5 people	30
4	Supervises work of more than 5 people	40

FACTOR C - EFFORT

Degree	Mentally Demanding	Points
1	No pressure; attention required at intervals	15
2	Frequent, but not continuous attention	20
3	Close attention required most of the time	25
4	High degree of concentration; close work	30

Degree	Physically Demanding	Points
1	Not significant	5
2	Frequent handling of lightweight materials	10
3	Intermittent lifting of heavy materials	15
4	Frequent or constant heavy, physical effort	20

APPENDIX O (*continued*)

FACTOR D - WORKING CONDITIONS

Degree	General Surroundings	Points
1	Works under desirable conditions	5
2	Conditions are only adequate	10
3	Intermittent unpleasant conditions	15
4	Continual high noise level or difficult situations	20

*Different point totals for various sub-factors, such as education, initiative, materials, etc., indicate different weights given to the respective sub-factors.

Source: Adapted from Sally A. Coltrin, *Study Guide, Readings and Exercises to Accompany Mathis and Jackson's Personnel—Contemporary Perspectives and Applications* (St. Paul, Minn.: West Publishing, 1979), pp. 216–19.

Bibliography

Aldag, R. J., and A. P. Brief. *Task Design*. Glenview, Ill.: Scott, Foresman, 1979.

American Management Association. *Book of Employment Forms*. New York: American Management Association, 1967.

Amrine, H. T., J. Ritchey, and D. S. Hulley. *Manufacturing Organization and Management*. Englewood Cliffs, N.J.: Prentice-Hall, 1975.

Anderson, Gary, Jerry Newman, and Frank Krzystofiak. "A Quantitative Approach to Measurement of Job Content: Procedures and Payoffs." *Personnel Psychology* 32 (1979), pp. 341-57.

Archer, W. B. *Computation of Group Job Descriptions from Occupational Survey Data*. San Antonio, Tex.: USAF, Personnel Research Laboratory, 1966.

Arvey, R. D., and K. M. Mossholder. "A Proposed Methodology for Determining Similarities and Differences Among Jobs." *Personnel Psychology* 30 (1977), pp. 363-74.

Bass, Bernard M., and Gerald V. Barrett. *Man, Work and Organizations*. Boston, Mass.: Allyn and Bacon, 1972.

Baum, Bernard H., and Peter F. Sorenson, Jr. "A Total Approach to Job Classification." *Personnel Journal*, January 1969, pp. 31-32.

Beatty, Richard W., and Craig Schneier. *Personnel Administration: An Experiential/Skill-Building Approach*. Reading, Mass.: Addison-Wesley, 1977.

Belcher, D. W. *Compensation Administration*. Englewood Cliffs, N.J.: Prentice-Hall, 1974.

Benge, Eugene J. "By-Products of Job Evaluation." *Personnel Journal*, July-August 1950, pp. 94-99.

Berenson, Conrad, and Henry O. Ruhnke. "Job Descriptions. Guidelines for Personnel Management." *Personnel Journal*, January 1966, pp. 14-19.

Brandt, Alfred R. "Describing Hourly Jobs." *Handbook of Wage and Salary Administration*. New York: McGraw-Hill, 1972.

Carrell, Michael R., and J. E. Dittrich. "Employee Perceptions of Fair Treatment." *Personnel Journal*, October 1976, pp. 523-24.

Carrell, Michael R., and Frank E. Kuzmits. *Personnel*. Columbus, Ohio: Charles E. Merrill, 1982.

Cascio, W. F., and H. Bernadin. "Implications of Performance Appraisal Litigation for Personnel Decisions." *Personnel Psychology* 34 (1981), pp. 211–26.

Christal, R. E., and J. J. Weissmuller. *New Comprehensive Occupational Data Analysis Programs for Analyzing Task Factor Information*. Lackland Air Force Base, Tex.: Air Force Human Resources Laboratory, 1976.

Cleavelin, Clifford C. "What's In a Job Title?" *The Management Review*, January 1959, pp. 56–57.

Cornelius, E. T., T. J. Carrar, and M. M. Collins. "Job Analysis Models and Job Classification." *Personnel Psychology* 32 (1979), pp. 693–708.

Davis, Louis E., and A. B. Cherns (eds.). *The Quality of Working Life*. New York: The Free Press, 1975.

Dessler, Gary. *Personnel Management*. Reston, Va: Reston Publishing Co., 1978.

Dunham, R. B. "The Measurement and Dimensionality of Job Characteristics." *Journal of Applied Psychology* 61 (1976), pp. 404–9.

Dunnette, M. D., L. M. Hough, and R. L. Rosse. "Task and Job Taxonomies as a Basis for Identifying Labor Supply Sources and Evaluating Employment Qualifications." *Affirmative Action Planning*. New York: Human Resource Planning Society, 1979, pp. 37–51.

Farrell, W. T., C. H. Stone, and D. Yoder. "Guidelines for Sampling in Marine Corps Task Analysis." *Evaluation of Marine Corps Task Analysis Program*, TR No. 11. Los Angeles: California State University, 1976.

Fine, Sidney. "Functional Job Analysis: An Approach to a Technology for Manpower Planning." *Personnel Journal*, November 1974, pp. 813–18.

———. *Functional Job Analysis Scales: A Desk Aid*. Kalamazoo, Mich.: Upjohn Institute for Employment Research, 1973.

Flanagan, J. C. "The Critical Incident Technique." *Psychological Bulletin* 51(1954), pp. 327–58.

Gambert, William. *A Trade Union Analysis of Time Study*. Englewood Cliffs, N.J.: Prentice-Hall, 1955.

Gehm, John W. "Job Descriptions—A New Handle on an Old Tool." *Personnel Journal*, December 1970, pp. 983–85.

Grant, Philip C. *Employee Motivation: Principles and Practices*. New York: Vantage Press, 1984.

———. "Managing By Task Inventories." *Management Solutions*, December 1987, pp. 4–13.

———. *The Performance Management Process*. Dubuque, Ia: Kendall/Hunt Publishing Co., 1986.

———. "What Use Is a Job Description?" *Personnel Journal*, February 1988, pp. 44–53.

———. "Why Job Descriptions Don't Work." *Personnel Journal*, January 1988, pp. 52–59.

———. Unpublished study of job descriptions used in 60 different Eastern Maine businesses, spring 1987.

Guian, Robert M. "Recruiting, Selection, and Job Placement." *Handbook of Industrial and Organizational Psychology*. Chicago: Rand McNally, 1976.

Hackman, J. R. "The Design of Work in the 1980s." *Organizational Dynamics*, Summer 1979, pp. 3–17.

Hackman, J. R., and G. R. Oldham. "Motivation through the Design of Work: Test of a Theory." *Organizational Behavior and Human Performance*, 16 (August 1976), pp. 250–79.

_____. *Work Redesign*. Reading, Mass.: Addison-Wesley, 1980.

Hazel, J. T., J. M. Madden, and R. E. Christal. "Agreement Between Worker-Supervisor Descriptions of the Worker's Job." *Journal of Industrial Psychology* 2 (1964), pp. 71–79.

Henderson, Richard I. *Compensation Management: Rewarding Performance*. Reston, Va.: Reston Publishing Co., 1979.

Hills, Frederick S. "Job Relatedness vs. Adverse Impact in Personnel Design Making." *Personnel Journal*, March 1980, pp. 211–15.

"How to Analyze Jobs." Bureau of Law and Business. Stamford, Conn.: Bureau of Law and Business, 1982.

"How to Write Job Descriptions the Right Way." Bureau of Law and Business. Stamford, Conn.: Bureau of Law and Business, 1982.

"Is Your Ablest Assistant Locked in Your Desk?" *Business Management*, November 1967, pp. 57–58.

Jacques, E. *Measurement of Responsibility*. New York: John Wiley, 1972.

_____. *Time-Span Handbook*. London: Heineman, 1964.

Jenkins, G. Douglas, David A. Nadler, Edward E. Lawler III, and Cortlandt Cammann. "Standardized Observations: An Approach to Measuring the Nature of Jobs." *Journal of Applied Psychology* 60 (1975), pp. 171–81.

"Job Description: Key to Hiring Right Man." *Industry Week*, April 10, 1972, pp. 61–62.

Jones, Jean J. Jr., and Thomas A. DeCottis. "Job Analysis: National Survey Findings." *Personnel Journal*, October 1969, pp. 805–9.

Jones, M. A. "Job Descriptions Made Easy." *Personnel Journal*, May 1984, pp. 31–34.

Kershner, A. M. *A Report on Job Analysis*. Washington, D.C.: Office of Naval Research, ONR Report ACR-5, 1955.

Klingner, Donald. "When the Traditional Job Description Is Not Enough." *Personnel Journal*, April 1979, pp. 243–48.

Lacy, John. "Job Evaluation and EEO." *Employee Relations Law Journal* 7, no. 3 (1979), pp. 210–17.

Lawler, E. E. "Job Design and Employee Motivation." *Personnel Psychology*, 22 (Winter 1969), pp. 415–44.

Lawshe, C. H. *Psychology of Industrial Relations*. New York: McGraw-Hill, 1953.

Levine, Edward L., Ronald A. Ash, Hardy Hall, and Frank Sistrunk. "Evaluation of Job Analysis Methods by Experienced Job Analysts." *Academy of Management Journal* 28, no. 1 (1983), pp. 339–48.

Likert, R. *New Patterns of Management*. New York: McGraw-Hill, 1961.

Livernash, E. Robert. "Internal Wage Structure." *New Concepts in Wage Determination*. New York: McGraw-Hill, 1957.

Maker, John R. (ed.). *New Perspectives in Job Environment*. New York: Van Nostrand Reinhold, 1971.

Markowitz, J. "Four Methods of Job Analysis." *Training and Development Journal*, September 1981, pp. 112–21.

McCormick, E. J. *Job Analysis: Methods and Applications*. New York: AMACOM, 1979.

_____. "Job and Task Analysis." *Handbook of Industrial and Organizational Psychology*. Chicago: Rand McNally, 1976.

_____. "Job Information: Its Development and Applications." *Handbook of Personnel and Industrial Relations.* Washington, D.C.: Bureau of National Affairs, 1979.

McCormick, E. J., J. W. Cunningham, and G. C. Gordon. "Job Dimensions Based on Factorial Analyses of Worker-Oriented Job Variables." *Personnel Psychology* 20 (1967), pp. 417–30.

McCormick, E. J., R. H. Finn, and C. D. Scheips. "Patterns of Job Requirements." *Journal of Applied Psychology* 41 (1957), pp. 358–65.

McCormick, E. J., P. R. Jeanneret, and R. C. Mecham. *The Development and Background of the Position Analysis Questionnaire.* West Lafayette, Ind.: Occupational Research Center, Purdue University, 1969.

Mescon, Michael H., and Donald O. Jewell. "The Position Description as a Communication Link." *Atlantic Economic Review*, January-February 1975, pp. 31–33.

Meyer, H. H. "Comparison of Foreman and General Foreman Conceptions of the Foreman's Job Responsibility." *Personnel Psychology* 12 (1959), pp. 445–52.

Milkovich, George T., and Charles Cogill. *Handbook of Wage and Salary Administration.* New York: McGraw-Hill, 1984.

Milkovich, George T., and Jerry M. Newman. *Compensation.* Plano, Tex.: Business Publications, 1984.

Morsh, J. E. "Job Analysis in the United States Air Force." *Personnel Psychology* 17, no. 17 (1964), pp. 7–17.

O'Reilly, Charles, G. N. Parlette, and J. Blum. "Perceptual Measures of Task Characteristics: The Biasing Effects of Differing Frames of Reference and Job Attitudes." *Academy of Management Journal* 123, no. 1 (1980), pp. 118–31.

Otteman, Robert, and J. Brad Chapman. "A Viable Strategy for Validation: Content Validity." *The Personnel Administrator*, November 1977, pp. 17–22.

Paterson, T. T., and T. M. Husband. "Decision-Making Responsibility: Yardstick for Job Evaluation." *Compensation Review*, Second Quarter 1970, pp. 21–31.

Pearlman, K. "Job Families: A Review and Discussion of Their Implications for Personnel Selection." *Psychological Bulletin* 87 (1980), pp. 1–28.

Pierce, J. L., and R. B. Dunham. "The Measurement of Perceived Job Characteristics: The Job Diagnostic Survey Versus the Job Characteristics Inventory." *Academy of Management Journal* 21, no. 1 (1978), pp. 123–28.

Prien, Erich P., and William N. Roman. "Job Analysis: A Review of Research Findings." *Personnel Psychology* 24 (1971), pp. 371–96.

Purves, Dale. "How to Write and Use Management Job Descriptions." *The Office*, January 1966, pp. 144–45.

Risher, Howard. "Job Analysis: A Management Perspective." *Employee Relations Law Journal* 4, no. 4 (1979), pp. 535–51.

Rush, H. M. *Job Design for Motivation.* New York: The Conference Board, 1972.

Russell, Richard S. "How Do You Describe a Job?" *Supervisory Management*, December 1959, pp. 15–19.

Sheibar, Paul. "A Simple Selection System Called Job Match." *Personnel Journal*, January 1979, p. 26.

Schuler, Randall S. *Personnel and Human Resource Management.* St. Paul: West Publishing, 1987.

Smith, Jack E., and Milton D. Hakel. "Convergence Among Data Sources, Response Bias, and Reliability and Validity of a Structured Job Analysis Questionnaire." *Personnel Psychology* 32, no. 4 (1979), pp. 677–92.

Sparks, Paul. "Job Analysis." *Personnel Management*. Boston: Allyn and Bacon, 1982.

Stimmler, Paul T. "The Job Evaluation Myth." *Personnel Journal*, November 1966, pp. 594–96.

Stone, C. H., and D. Yoder. *Job Analysis*. Long Beach: California State College, 1970.

Suojanen, W. W., G. L. Swallow, and M. J. McDonald. *Perspectives on Job Enrichment and Productivity*. Atlanta: Georgia State University, 1975.

Suskin, Harold. "Job Evaluation—It's More than a Tool for Setting Pay Rates." *Public Personnel Review*, October 1970, pp. 283–89.

Sutermeister, Robert A. (ed.). *People and Productivity*. New York: McGraw-Hill, 1969.

Teske, Sidney, and Ernest Johnson. *Programmed Study Guide for Job Analysis Training Course*. Washington, D.C.: U.S. Government Printing Office, 1978.

Tornow, Walter, and Patrick Pinto. "The Development of a Managerial Job Taxonomy: A System for Describing, Classifying and Evaluating Executive Office Positions." *Journal of Applied Psychology* 61 (1976), pp. 410–18.

Umstot, D. D., C. H. Bell, and T. R. Mitchell. "Effects of Job Enrichment and Task Goals on Satisfaction and Productivity: Implications for Job Design." *Journal of Applied Psychology*, 61 (August 1976), pp. 379–94.

United States Civil Service Commission. *Job Analysis*. Washington, D.C.: U.S. Government Printing Office, December 1976.

_____.*Job Analysis: A Guide for State and Local Governments*. Washington, D.C.: Bureau of Intergovernmental Personnel Programs, 1973.

_____.*Job Analysis: Developing and Documenting Data*. Washington, D.C.: Bureau of Intergovernmental Personnel Programs, 1973.

_____.*Job Analysis: Developing and Documenting Data, A Guide for State and Local Governments*. Washington, D.C.: U.S. Government Printing Office, 1973.

_____.*Job Analysis: Key to Better Management*. Washington, D.C.: U.S. Government Printing Office, 1973.

U.S. Department of Labor, Manpower Administration. *Handbook for Analyzing Jobs*. Washington, D.C.: U.S. Government Printing Office, 1972.

United States Training and Employment Service. *Dictionary of Occupational Titles*. Washington, D.C.: U.S. Government Printing Office, 1965.

Walsh, William J. "Writing Job Descriptions: How and Why." *Supervisory Management*, February 1972, pp. 2–8.

Wendt, George R. "Should Courts Write Your Job Descriptions?" *Personnel Journal*, September 1976, pp. 442–445.

Yoder, D., and H. G. Heneman, Jr. (eds.). *ASPA, Handbook of Personnel and Industrial Relations*. Washington, D.C.: Bureau of National Affairs, 1979.

Zollitsch, Herbert G., and Adolph Langsner. *Wage and Salary Administration*, Cincinnati: Southwestern Publishing, 1970.

Index

About the Author

PHILIP C. GRANT is Professor of Management at Husson College, Bangor, Maine, and President of Supervisory Training Associates, a consulting firm specializing in human resources management. His more than 60 published articles have appeared in journals such as *Personnel, Personnel Journal,* and *Personnel Administrator.* He is also author of two previous books, *Employee Motivation: Principles and Practices* and *The Performance Management Process.*